END-TIME DELIVERANCE

and the
HOLY SPIRIT REVIVAL!

THE NEW THING THAT GOD IS DOING IN THE EARTH

PETER HOBSON

1st Edition   1984
2nd Edition   1989
3rd Edition   1995

National Library of Australia
I.S.B.N. 0 646 27530 5

Printed in Sri Lanka

Publisher:
Bethlehem House
Kuala Lumpur
Malaysia

To—

The people of Full Salvation Fellowship who are the Lord's courageous pioneers of a mighty new thrust of His Holy Spirit.

With no encouragement from the Church (but the reverse) they have believed the Word of God rather than the unbelief of many students of the Word of God. As a reward of their faith, they are being changed from glory to glory! Hallelujah!

CONTENTS

PREFACE to the SECOND EDITION

What is the Deliverance Ministry all about? Why has it been restored to the Body of Christ in these **End-Times**?

This is not a book which tells you HOW but a book which tells you **WHY** and **WHERE** and **WHAT is happening.**

It is not really about **methods** of deliverance, although there is some insight into group ministry, but it will give the Born Again Christian who eagerly awaits the appearance of King Jesus a strong sense of PURPOSE and DIRECTION as they get themselves ready for Him.

In other words **it will give YOU God's perfect will for you (WHY), WHAT is happening TODAY in these END-TIMES and the way to go (WHERE).** What more can you ask? HOW (methods) are detailed in our series on Christian Deliverance, books 1 to 4.

May we remind you of a very important discovery by the famous **Louis Pasteur** (1822-95). Amongst his many scientific achievements Pasteur discovered that most diseases are caused by **specific germs** (micro-organisms). After suffering much ridicule he was able to show that the putrefaction in wine, beer, milk, alcohol and other liquids was caused by germs or micro-organisms, which are not spontaneously generated by the putrefaction processes themselves, as had been previously thought, but are found in the air to which the affected substances have been previously exposed. His subsequent investigations of anthrax and rabies further validated his theories and resulted in the prevention and cure of these and many other diseases in men and animals. Pasteur thus proved the germ theory of disease and founded the science of immunology.

Imagine! Man discovering that **disease is caused by thousands or even millions of tiny little creatures,** invisible to the naked eye, which are packed into the human body (or small part of a body) and cause its woes! No wonder they laughed at him—until tests, experience and results proved him right! Now transfer this TRUE story from history—and its lesson—out of the physical realm into the spiritual realm and ponder it. Should you run into any difficulties while reading this book, especially in the chapter exposing the extent of human demonisation, please remember Louis Pasteur, and then continue. Thank you.

Peter Hobson
Crows Nest
December 1983

PREFACE to the THIRD EDITION

Even as I prepare the third edition of this book **there is a move of God's Spirit sweeping the Body of Christ in many parts of the world.** It is characterised by God's people breaking out into "uncontrollable" laughter, shaking, roaring, deliverances and healings. Many people affected end up on the ground under the power of God and when they arise later they witness to the refreshment the Lord has given them.

This movement is sometimes called the **Toronto Blessing** because the **Vineyard Church at Toronto Airport** has been a prime source of the movement spreading internationally. Some say it began in South Africa, some in South America, but all that doesn't really matter.

What matters is that this sovereign move of the Holy Spirit makes this book more important than ever. Indeed I am bold to say that **End-Time Deliverance is the PRIMARY purpose of this mighty move**, and all other reasons (benefits) come second, even the refreshment of the saints.

At the end of reading this book you should have a lot of your questions about the Holy Spirit (Toronto?) blessing answered for you, especially WHY? and WHAT FOR? As I write people are running (flying, etc.) from all over the world to receive from, be touched by and refreshed by the Holy Spirit. The movement is in its HONEYMOON stage. (It should soon move into the TEACHING stage, which will feature THEOLOGICAL WARFARE between the Pharisees (cf. Matt. 23:24) and the People of the Spirit, the Foolish and the Wise, the indulgent and the crucified with Christ.

Will Christians also run in like manner to be CLEANSED FROM ALL POLLUTION OF FLESH AND OF SPIRIT, PERFECTING HOLINESS IN THE FEAR OF GOD? (2 Cor. 7:1). When we see this happening we will know the Lord is moving us into the fourth and final stage before the Rapture—the purifying of the Bride of Christ!

Perhaps the problem does not lie so much with the flock of God but with the shepherds of the flocks. I believe the Lord God Almighty is sick and tired of waiting for His shepherds to begin cleansing programs for His people so they can make themselves ready for the Bridegroom. For too long His Pastors have fiddled and fuddled about with Church growth programs and empire-building (supposedly for the glory of Christ) and unintentionally, unknowingly neglected the innermost spiritual needs of their people—and themselves!

All that has to change now. They can still fiddle around with this present move of the Spirit. They can use it as a gimmick to fill their churches, or promote themselves, in which cases they will never get past the honeymoon stage of the movement. Or they can call on their **Deliverance Ministers to get down to the Lord's business** when the power of God falls, and begin the massive clean up operation the Lord wants done on and in His Body—the people of God.

The Vision, simply stated, is:
>   ... **the perfecting of the saints** (believers)
>   ... **to the measure of the stature of the fullness of Christ** (Eph. 4:12-13)
>   ... **through spiritual (inner) cleansing** (James 4:8; 2 Peter 3:13-14)

... by Deliverance and Restoration programs
(Rom. 12:2; 2 Cor. 7:1)
... in the Name of the Lord Jesus Christ (Col. 3:17).

The weaponry of the Holy Spirit to get the job done is now available (has been, for years). I pray that after you have read this book you will experience it (Him) to the fullest!

Peter Hobson
Crows Nest
N.S.W. Australia
February, 1995

END-TIME DELIVERANCE

INTRODUCTION

The Deliverance Ministry of Christ (casting out demons) is not something people relish for themselves. They usually try every other avenue or solution in order to solve their emotional and/or mental problems, but finally—when nothing else works—some Christians, perhaps braver than the others (or perhaps more desperate) finally yield themselves into the hands of a deliverance minister, because they think that what they are **about** to go through cannot be as bad as what they have **been** going through.

However, thousands (perhaps representing a very large percentage of all Christians) prefer to put up with their bondages because they are not quite desperate enough and view the medicine of "exorcism", as it is unfortunately often called, as probably worse than the infirmity they bear, and consequently do nothing effective.

Perhaps you are one of those Christians who knows deep down in your spirit that you need the ministry of deliverance, but the thought of private sessions during the week with lots of yelling (by the minister) and possible screaming and other manifestations (from yourself) —the noise, humiliation and potential ugliness all seems just too much to handle—even to think about, especially as some sessions can go on for hours with everybody ending up exhausted spiritually, emotionally and physically. The prospect of having to receive ministry over a series of such sessions is not very inviting and with this kind of deliverance set-up **the medicine can seem worse than the affliction!**

However, praise God,

I want to say now, LOUDLY and CLEARLY, that for 9 out of 10 people, deliverance doesn't have to be like that. Let me say that again,

IT DOESN'T HAVE TO BE LIKE THAT.

Needful people can get deliverance as the Spirit moves through a congregation—

–AS YOU PRAISE AND WORSHIP the Lord
–AS YOU LISTEN to Bible messages
–and AS YOU PRAY—
all in fellowship with other Christians.

Through sheer pressure of time (and it can be so time consuming) and weight of experience, we have been taught of the Lord a whole new concept in deliverance where whole congregations can receive ministry in the course of normal worship and praise meetings; and where, as the Spirit moves over the whole assembly touching this one here and that one there according to His sovereignty, He leads the deliverance minister(s) and gives a word of knowledge and discernment of spirits etc. wherever necessary.

This methodology for the deliverance ministry is not really the subject of this book but suffice to say here that it is simply a combination of a normal worship meeting on the one hand, with Praise, Prayer and Preaching, and a Deliverance session on the other. The deliverance commands are simply given at the beginning of the meeting (with other appropriate prayers) and issued as necessary, throughout, until everything is sealed off with further commands and prayers at the end of the meeting. Obviously in such meetings unconverted people should be encouraged to make up their minds to either accept or reject the Lord Jesus—even perhaps to get converted or move out. We normally lead the assembly in a type of "sinners' prayer"[1] at the beginning of our meetings, and it includes a request for healing and deliverance also, so that everyone present has the opportunity to open up their hearts to the Holy Spirit's searching ministry. In any event when the Risen Lord is present in power to heal and to deliver, your meetings will be no place for hypocrites to want to hang around. In other words you can get your deliverance during your normal weekly worship at the same time as many others around you and no extra hours of private ministry are required.

If you say: "Hey, that sounds great!", then let me tell you more good news. **That is how we believe that the Lord wants EVERY faithful fellowship to operate in this last hour.** That is the way He has taught us and that is what we are sharing with Christian leaders who have ears to hear, hearts of shepherd's love and the faith to act.

Not only is this method easier and more simple for both subject and minister alike but it is **the only way the massive clean-up work of God can take place in the time available.** Only recently I read where an alive assembly performs an average of ONE (1) "exorcism" a week. But as that church probably increases its congregation by at least 20 new members every week its

---

[1] Curse-breaking, plus yielding and commitment

"exorcism" program is actually going backwards. The widespread need of deliverance ministry will become more apparent as this book is studied and **the present methods used in most assemblies will stand revealed as totally inadequate.**

For example, according to a report in a Sydney newspaper[1] both **Roman Catholic** and **Pentecostal** spokesmen say that the ministry **"is only performed in extreme cases"**, while the **Anglicans** don't even want to talk about it! However the truth is that most Christians are now "extreme cases" because if we don't get our lives (spirits, souls and bodies) put right BEFORE the Lord comes for us **we will end up like the five (5) foolish maidens (virgins)** who had the door of the wedding feast with Jesus shut in their faces.

I expect to show beyond a shadow of a doubt that the need is not minor, it is MAJOR and it is URGENT, for now is the time for the Full Salvation of God to be revealed, and it will challenge and expose the innermost motives and commitment of EVERY human being who calls himself or herself Christian.

I have taken the trouble to explain the changes in methodology for deliverance in order to REMOVE the present notion that people sometimes have in their minds about deliverance being a hard and unpleasant course. It has its difficulties and testings but there is no need to be afraid; and remember, **it is performed by the Spirit of God and the kingdom of God comes upon you to the glory of the Lord Jesus,** who set His face upon an even harder road, even to die on a crude, wooden cross

---

[1] "Sydney Morning Herald" Nov/Dec. 1983

in order to defeat all your enemies and to redeem your life from the Pit, and who now invites you to enter even more into His victory with joy and thanksgiving.

Please do not expect to find every section in this book easy reading. **"End-Time Deliverance" is a theological subject grounded in the Word of God,** and as such not every point may be quickly and easily grasped. But do please persevere. If the meaning of one section eludes you please press on in faith, because I believe there is enough scriptural evidence, both plain and profound, to satisfy most Bible students. Certainly it is my earnest prayer that you the reader will not only find this study profitable but that you will also catch the vision, and move into it.

> "Thou waitest for deliverance,
> O soul thou waitest long!
> Believe that NOW deliverance
> Doth wait for thee in song!"

> "Sigh not until deliverance
> Thy fettered soul doth free;
> With songs of glad deliverance
> God NOW doth compass thee."
> Author Unknown

CHAPTER 1

A VISION FOR THE END-TIME

(i) THE BRIDEGROOM AND THE BRIDE

The time is short. The world is in big trouble and Jesus is coming for a beautiful Bride—the universal church. Unfortunately, if He came today, He would be marrying a very troubled, divided (double-minded), unclean "lady"—inwardly an ugly hag[1] who has committed adultery with the world. It is God's time for the big clean-up. The Bride must make herself ready (Rev. 19:7).

"But", you say, "the Bride IS beautiful. Her sins have been atoned for by the shedding of the Blood of the Lamb of God and the church is now clothed with the righteousness of Christ. She is justified by faith and has put on Christ. Her robes are white, washed in the Blood of the Lamb!"

And all that is true—Praise the Lord it is true. **She looks beautiful on the outside.** But may I take the men readers back to when they were young and single. How many beautiful girls there seemed to be, and life was full of interest as you sought to make friends with the fair sex. In the first instance you were attracted by the outward appearance, but you were too wise to be satisfied with just skin-deep beauty.

---

[1] Concept voiced by Dr. Derek Prince, cassette tape DP 15, unwelcome but true.

As you talked some of you became disenchanted when the sweet young thing opened her mouth and spoke her first words in your hearing. With others you found that she smoked and you really could taste the difference. Yet others were frivolous and only chased a "good" time, wanting your money spent on them. Some were promiscuous, and played the harlot and could not be trusted.

And all the time you were looking for a girl who was not only beautiful IN YOUR EYES, but one with whom you felt comfortable, relaxed and good inside, because she had moral standards and a pure, warm and joyful heart. You could trust her because of her fidelity to YOU, and her standards of right and wrong earned your respect. If you found such a girl you probably wanted to marry her, but basically you wanted someone like yourself, someone compatible with yourself on the fundamental issues of life. Of course, many of these principles are looked for by the ladies also, when being courted by men.

These things are what Jesus the Bridegroom wants in His Bride, the Church. Outward beauty alone is inadequate. He wants a Bride who not only has been forgiven for her sins but who has "died to sin", and has ceased from sin, the ROOT, SPIRITUAL disease of the human heart. He wants a Bride who is without spot or blemish, like Himself. He wants a Bride who is "all glorious within", a Bride with a pure heart, full of the Holy Spirit, faithful to her fiancé/husband and with whom He is comfortable and relaxed (humanly speaking), compatible in mind and character because together they are one in Spirit and total communion. In short, **He wants a Bride LIKE HIMSELF.**

Do not the scriptures tell us that we are to have the

mind of Christ (which is spiritual, heavenly, not of the earth) and we should be transformed by the renewing of our fleshly carnal minds and be conformed to the image of the Son of God? (Rom. 12:2). Does not God's Word promise us that **when we see Him, we shall be like Him** (1 John 3:2) and **blessed are the pure in heart for they shall see God** (Matt. 5:8)?

How does the Bride measure up right now? As we implied before, if the Lord Jesus were to come and marry her now, He would soon discover what many men (and women) have already discovered to their sorrow—that (outward) beauty is indeed only skin deep, covering in part and to some extent the heart of a witch. For the Lord Jesus to marry such a Bride is unthinkable!

(ii) PURSUING CHRISTLIKENESS

It takes maybe forty (40) years for a Christian to be changed from an "average" sinner into someone whose conduct is identifiable as being that of a saint. Theoretically and legally we become saints of God when we are born again because we are separated from the World and set apart for God's purposes at that point. However **it takes quite a while, perhaps a lifetime, for our transformation and conduct as a Christian to even appear to catch up with our legal position in Christ**. Our sanctification (sainting, separation for God) is usually a lifetime process, and at the end of it few people will call us a saint in the sense of being a **Saint Paul** or **Saint Francis.**

Indeed most Christians seem to finish their lives disappointed with their efforts to serve the Lord. I once worked with a senior Christian minister who looked particularly glum one day. When I asked him what was troubling him, he said, "I've got to go and have dinner with the Archbishop tonight, to celebrate twenty-five years in the ministry". "Twenty-five years?" said I. "That's marvellous—praise the Lord!" "Yes", he said, "But what have I achieved?" He was genuinely reflecting back on a ministry that could have been, and should have been, but somehow never fulfilled its potential. This is not unusual. Sad to say, it is probably normal. All of us who are called to full-time service for the Lord want to do great things for Him. We may even see how our gifts could achieve great and Godly things, but somehow we are so hindered and obstructed, that before we know it, forty years has flashed by with our dreams and visions unfulfilled. Worse still, although sanctification has taken place to some extent and we appear to have grown in grace somewhat, nevertheless we find ourselves still chained with the same old besetting sins we had in our youth, although we may have become more expert in hiding them from other people.

However I now maintain that this End-Time period is going to be different for those who want to be different badly enough. **I see people IN REGULAR DELIVERANCE MINISTRY changing as much, if not more, in FOUR YEARS as many other Christians have changed in FORTY YEARS**, and I expect the transformation process through deliverance to shorten even further as the Lord's timetable advances and the End of the Age draws closer.

Does this sound great to you and are you praising the Lord? Good, but two words of caution:

(i) Even after forty years of sanctification we will

still seem to fall far short of the perfection of the Lord Jesus, and

(ii) Each Christian is, in the final analysis, responsible for their own rate of progress, according to their commitment, obedience (action) and submission (attitude).

What is the way forward? I repeat—it is God's time for the big clean-up. The Bride must make herself ready, but here we must make an important distinction between that part of the Bride which has already "died in Christ" and which shall rise first at the Rapture (1 Thess. 4:13-17) and those who are alive, i.e. who will not taste death but will be translated from earth to heaven while alive, perhaps in the manner of Enoch (Gen. 5:24) and/or Elijah (2 Kings 2:11). **It is THIS LATTER group—those Raptured ALIVE for which the inward cleansing has such special meaning,** and indeed what the Lord has so clearly begun to do today concerning the inner deliverance/cleansing of His people surely ANTICIPATES that the Rapture is not far away.

Are we getting into the "sticky" matter of Sinless Perfection? This was one of John Wesley's favourite views during the 18th century, but was opposed by the vast majority of leaders in the Body of Christ for three main reasons:

(i) a superficial explanation of 1 John 1:7-9.
(ii) the comfort that the doctrine of Justification by Faith afforded.
(iii) the disbelief that any human being could possibly achieve such a state in this life-time.

Can we be perfected BEFORE entering fully into the Kingdom of Heaven?

Maybe—maybe not. If it was attainable I would say that it is only attainable by ONE generation of Christians— those who will not taste death but will be CAUGHT UP ALIVE in the Rapture party (1 Thess. 4:13-17). For them the spiritual law that **the wages of sin is death** will not apply! (Rom. 6:23a).

What we can certainly say is that the Word of God commands us to "go for it!" Whether we are perfected or not—**go for it**[1]! Run the race to finish and receive your crown (1 Cor. 9:24-25). The good Lord will take care of the details! But someone will ask, "If I am IN Christ my life is hid 'in Him' and sin is not reckoned to me any more. I don't need inner cleansing because my sins are blotted out." As one clergyman put it, "What's all this business about being filled with the Spirit? **It's not that we have *Him* BUT THAT He has *us* that matters.**" But of course these propositions should not be in an "either...or" conflict. **They are not contradictory but complementary** and BOTH propositions are important to a Christian. Our life is indeed hid in Christ but His life indwells us also. Jesus said:

"In that day you will know that I am in my Father, and you in me and I in you." (John 14:20)

It is indefensible for Christians to rest on their conversion experience and the atoning sacrifice of the Lord Jesus Christ on Calvary's Cross and use their legal position of being justified by faith as an excuse to disobey

---

[1] See Appendix G for a fuller discussion.

the Lord's commands[1] to be cleansed and purified ˒ TER CONVERSION. If we ignore the Lord's commands in this matter we have moved into a position of DISO-BEDIENCE which, of course, none of us want to do, knowingly or unknowingly.

What we have to do is to capture for ourselves the heart of Christ in this matter which, of course, is the same as having the mind of Christ. **Colin Urquhart** is a Bible teacher of international repute who has earned the respect of Christians everywhere the hard way—by service to the Body of Christ, and he writes[2] about what he understands (by revelation) to be **the heart of Christ for His Church:**

*"...A great sense of the Lord's grief came upon me. He showed that it was **His Church, more than the lost,** that grieved Him. I found myself pleading before the throne of God for the churches of that area, crying out for Him to have mercy on His people. I **wanted to pray for all who didn't know the Lord, but the Spirit would not lift this burden of grief over the churches ...***

*...On one evening there were at least 300 people kneeling all over the place praying that the fire of God's Spirit would come upon them, **to purge and cleanse them from all that was unholy and to give them hearts that wanted to live in holy obedience to Him."***

Just think about this for a moment or two. What priority

---

[1] See Appendix D—"RESTORATION SCRIPTURES"
[2] "Faith for the Future"

would YOU attribute to the Lord when considering **(i)**
the salvation of the lost and **(ii) the cleansing of the
Church?** Here is a widely respected man of God who
says the Lord showed him that **the Church's condition
is EVEN MORE grieving to Him than the condition of
the lost.**

Food for thought indeed!

(iii) VICTORY OVER SIN

There is also confusion between SIN and SINS. The
Root of Sin in the heart CAUSES the sins we commit
in action (both sins of commission and omission). It is
the CAUSE and EFFECT principle. As Jesus said, sins
come out of (are sourced in) the heart of man, where
the causal **disease** of sin resides. Now, when we are
justified by faith[1] and the imputed righteousness of Christ
clothes us, SINS (the misdeeds) are truly blotted out,
but the shed Blood of the Lamb of God on Calvary has
yet another powerful victory and blessing to offer us.
The Blood of Christ obtained victory over all the powers
of darkness *including the disease of SIN in our hearts*
(John 1:29; Col. 2:8-15, 20; 1 John 1:7-9)

Clearly, **being justified by faith is the basis of ALL
our blessings in Christ,** and enables the dead in
Christ to rise first and be forever with the Lord (1 Thess.
4:16-17) bearing in mind that **when they died,** their
souls left their bodies. All that was unclean, i.e. every
unclean spirit in their souls, then had the task of

---

[1] The doctrine of being RECKONED or ACCOUNTED righteous because
of our faith (TRUST) in Christ.

re-incarnating[1] itself in whatever other body of flesh was available to it, while the human spirits were transferred to Paradise to be with the Lord to await the fulfilment of the Plan of the Ages.

However, in the case of those ALIVE when the Trumpet sounds, it is plain that, like **Enoch** and **Elijah,** they will **not experience death at all,** and since death is a consequence of sin (Gen. 3; Rom. 5:12-14, 21; 6:23) i.e. the SPIRITUAL disease of the human heart, it should come as no surprise to us that God should want to deal with this basic disease in those who will not obtain release of all the uncleanness in their souls through the event of physical death, i.e. BEFORE the Rapture event. One could argue that such uncleanness would leave the soul when our bodies are translated into spiritual bodies, at or just prior to the Rapture event, and my only answer to that is to take a leaf out of the apostle Paul's writings and say, "Who are you O man to answer back to God? Will what is moulded say to its moulder, 'Why have you made me thus?'" (Rom. 9:20). Similarly we would be saying to God, "Why have you acted thus, I thought you would do things my way?"

To my knowledge there are no scriptures which specify at precisely what point in time God is going to lift away the sin, the spiritual disease of the human heart, from within the alive children He is rapturing. One might THINK that it will be at the moment of Translation from this earthly realm to the spiritual realm, but there is no satisfactory evidence for this. It is a theory of convenience

---

[1] Unclean spirits re-incarnate themselves throughout history, but the HUMAN spirit only experiences the death of its body (house) once (Heb. 9:27). See Book 4 "Discerning Human Nature" for a full discussion.

because we have not previously known the details of the unfolding of the will of God in this matter, and it has seemed to fit the apostle Paul's explanation that **"we shall all be changed, in a moment, in the twinkling of an eye"** (1 Cor. 15:51-52)[1]. However even a superficial look at the context of this passage confirms that Paul is speaking about BODILY changes, viz.:

> v.35 with what kind of BODY do they come? (are they raised from the dead?)

> v.39 not all FLESH is alike...

> v.42 what is sown is perishable what is raised is IMPERISHABLE

> v.44 it is sown a PHYSICAL BODY, it is raised a SPIRITUAL BODY

> v.52 ...the dead will be raised IMPERISHABLE...

and so on.

Nothing in this passage could be said to support the notion that the SOUL undergoes an instant change of deliverance at the Rapture of the saints who remain alive. It has only to do with our bodily substance, being and appearance.

---

[1] Prophecy of J. Leland Earls, Word of Life Fellowship, Spokane USA published in "The Manifested Sons" Issue no. 3, 1967 confirms our position: "Immediately following shall a great host be instantly changed, in the twinkling of an eye, **as all those who have been prepared by me** and who have finished their course are caught up to be with the Lord (1 Cor. 15:51-54). Thus shall that glorious church, which has been the object and goal of this entire dispensation, be completed and joined with the Lord in the heavenlies..."

So we can underline again that the theory God will only cleanse the SOULS of His alive saints at the moment of their Translation to be with Jesus is quite unsupported in the Scriptures and is therefore unconvincing. On the contrary, the evidence gathered here presents a different view and can be summed up in the words of **John the Baptist:**

> *"Prepare ye the Way of the Lord—make His paths straight."*

—or in modern words—put right the things that are wrong in your life NOW! Get rid of the sin in your heart NOW! Submit yourself to the searching of His Spirit within you NOW!—and to His delivering Grace—NOW[1].

The apostle John puts it this way:

> *"Beloved, now we are children of God and it has not yet been shown what we shall be. We know that when He is manifested **we shall be like him,** because we shall see Him as He is.*
>
> *And everyone having this hope concerning Him **purifies himself as He is pure."***
>
> (1 John 3: 2-3).

Did you know, dear Christian, that when you see Jesus YOU WILL BE LIKE HIM?

Do you have this blessed hope? If you can say "Amen"

---

[1] Some scriptures expressing the need for Christians to be cleansed, purified, transformed, restored and conformed to the image of Christ are listed in Appendix D. The pursuit of PERFECTION is discussed in Appendix G.

to these two questions THEN the Scripture of John says that **YOU SHOULD BE PURIFYING YOURSELF to make yourself** (by God's Grace) **LIKE HIM, and you should be doing it NOW!** Amen?

Please note it doesn't say that because you are justified by faith and forgiven for your (misdeeds of) sins God will take out the (disease of) sin in your heart **AS you are being Raptured,** because you would not be involved in that at all, it would be a sovereign act of Grace, like the Rapture itself. But the apostle John says **YOU are involved.** YOU are involved in appropriating His Grace by the **purifying of yourself** (through deliverance, healing and sanctification) even as Jesus is pure so that when you do see Him, whether through death or Rapture, you will be like Him. Hallelujah!

(iv) A TIME OF REVELATION

Difficult to accept? Our understanding of this whole matter is based on two incontrovertible facts happening RIGHT NOW:

(i) **The revelation of the MAGNITUDE of human demonisation.**

(ii) **The DEEP and CONTINUOUS SEARCHING and ministry of the Holy Spirit into the hearts of those children of God who have asked for His deliverance.**

From these two magnificent revelations from the Lord, I for one am compelled to seek an understanding of the unfolding Will of God in these dramatic days, and this book is an attempt, in part, to seek, to know, to explain and to move with that WILL, and at the same time to untie a few spiritual knots about RESTORATION ministry. Certainly we know that the CONTINUOUS and DEEP cleansing of the souls of God's people began no later than 1973, only because that was when Verlie and I were brought into the action, so we must consider that the time remaining before the Rapture is short, although it seems that **the Body of Christ at large has not yet caught on to this vision.**

What is the Vision again? (from the Preface to the Third Edition)

The Vision, simply stated is,

> ... **the perfecting of the saints** (believers)
> ... **to the measure of the stature of the fullness of Christ** (Eph. 4:12-13)
> ... **through spiritual (inner) cleansing** (James 4:8; 2 Peter 3:13-14)
> ... **by Deliverance and Restoration programs** (Rom. 12:2; 2 Cor. 7:1)
> ... **in the Name of the Lord Jesus Christ** (Col. 3:17).

—or, if you want it stated in one proof text from the Word of God:

"Let us CLEANSE OURSELVES FROM ALL POL-LUTION OF FLESH AND OF SPIRIT, perfecting holiness, in the fear of God". (2 Cor. 7:1)

The Body of Christ may not be in tune yet, but it is **the Body of Christ** which will also produce the **Bride of Christ**[1] and MUST be awakened (or at least 50% of her

---

[1] Please study a comparison between the Body of Christ and the Bride of Christ in Appendix E.

—Matt. 25:1-13). She is already clothed with the righteous clothing of Jesus on the outside, being justified by faith, but NOW is the time for her cleansing in the inward parts. NOW is the full and great salvation of our God ready to be revealed, that the Bride might truly be without spot or blemish for her Lord.

This truth will greatly affect every minister and ministry now in operation in the church. Indeed, deliverance ministries, although facing enormous negative and unclean forces from within the Body of Christ herself at the time of writing, *will become the prevailing emphasis, together with evangelism,* right up to the Rapture of believers because the Lord Jesus Christ is coming for a beautiful girl, inside and outside.

Why will this affect all ministers and ministries? Simply because Christians coming for deliverance from temporal and external problems of an isolated nature *now* find themselves coming under the searching scrutiny of God's Holy Spirit for *all manner* of mental, emotional and physical uncleanness. This has been our experience since we were called to this ministry. After Verlie had ministered quickly and effectively against a **nicotine** kingdom one day and likewise myself against an **epileptic** kingdom another day, our next major case (in 1973) was to a Deaconess with a spirit of **fear.** When we commanded it to come out in Jesus' Name, the sister's head began to twist violently from side to side, so much that I was concerned that she would cause herself an injury. However, the demon quickly left, and, not having anything more than a superficial understanding of what God's Word has to say about deliverance, although I thought I had made a reasonably sound study of the subject, I assumed the matter was closed and total victory had been won.

Imagine my surprise therefore when the same sister returned three months later requesting further ministry. I knew that other ministries would have told her that she had let the demon back in through lack of faith or lack of commitment or ungodly conduct, but I knew that none of these explanations was true—it wasn't her fault at all. If anything it was my fault because I had been deceived by the current theological trends of the day, that of believing the old *"there's only one spirit—get that out and you're right—easy, instant deliverance for all"* trick. When I look back on it now I am amazed at my naivety about spiritual warfare. That day we removed a further eleven strong spirits from the lass and we didn't stop ministering until we were sure that all manifestations had ceased. From that day we have encouraged many sufferers to accept **continuous ministry** in order that we may monitor as careful a follow-up system as is humanly possible, in order that no ugly thing shall escape detection and expulsion. **Slap-happy, "near enough" optimism that is mistakenly labelled "faith" is just not good enough for a salvation ministry.**

In some cases **unbelief, life-style** and **habits,** etc. MAY be the reason for continuing problems, but in my experience the vast majority of continuing problems indicate, not failure by the subject, but simply that the Ministry has only removed the tip of the ice-berg. An ice-berg manifests one-ninth of its substance above the ocean where it can be seen while eight-ninths remain submerged. However, if we were to remove the visible ninth from the top that would not mean that the iceberg would become invisible, with its whole mass below the surface. No, the ice-berg would adjust itself so that even though it was smaller now, one-ninth would appear above and eight-ninths below the waves. The laws of nature are such that we only ever see one-ninth of the total danger manifesting itself in normal conditions—not more and not less. The proportions may be different, but **sin is like that** and **unclean spirits are like that,** and these are the subject matter of other books[1] in which the nature of sin, unclean spirits, *the old man* and *the man of sin,* etc. are discussed, but for now it is important to accept the principle that spasmodic, once-every-five-years deliverance is not even scratching the surface of the ice-berg of problems in Christians.

As our case history experience increased we discovered that when the Lord has removed a particular kingdom of spirits out of a sufferer, before the sufferer could pack up and go home, they would begin to manifest another type of spirit and need to start all over again. Many people were delivered of as many as a dozen different kinds of spirits and we began to realise that the Holy Spirit was no longer content to minister to obvious and spectacular problems only but was desirous of digging deep into the hidden, inner parts of man and woman, where all the **hereditary roots** and **childhood scars** had left their "indelible" mark upon the human personality.

Let me make one thing very clear. We did NOT set out just to make a lot of work for ourselves, in Christ. We are not seeking to build a dependency upon our ministry—that is, seeking our own glory and exaltation. Such motives would be unworthy of any Christian, reprehensible and doomed to failure from the beginning, for the Lord brings down the proud and exalts the humble and

---

[1] Christian Deliverance Book 4 **"Discerning Human Nature"** or **"Your Full Salvation"**

meek, of which we are well aware. NO, IT IS NECES-SARY for Christians to receive CONTINUOUS MINI-STRY today. That is our experience, supported by the Word of God, as we intend to show.

It would be idle for you or me to say "I'm not interested in big volume work: I just want to help the odd person (no pun intended) in need in our assembly." I thought so too, at the beginning, because I thought that the ministry today had the same impetus and objects that Jesus' ministry had nineteen centuries ago.

(v) THE REAL RENEWAL

But there is **a very big difference**. Jesus ministered then as a demonstration of his compassion, power and the Kingdom of God which He preached. **It was a ministry to external problems of an obvious nature**—things which stood out as the works of the devil. Today the Lord is preparing His people with an inner cleansing from the problems which exist deep within the inner person, where they are not so obvious. Indeed **it is the hidden problems NOT obvious to men but seen by God alone that the Holy Spirit is searching out today, that the Bride of Christ might be truly without spot or blemish when the Bridegroom comes for her. THIS is the Great Salvation ready to be revealed in the last time** (1 Peter 1:5) and there will be ONE GENERATION of the Bride (Church) so cleansed—the generation that is caught up in the air to meet the Lord! (1 Thess. 4:17). She will not only be **"without spot or wrinkle"** to look at but also **"all glorious within"** (Ps. 45:13 KJV). She will be without spot or wrinkle, both legally AND experientially (Eph. 5:26-27; 2 Peter 3:11-14).

24

This is her high calling from God, her goal, her aim.
God's purposes for the ministry have not changed since
Jesus' earthly walk but now they are more urgent, more
far-reaching and more openly revealed in God's Plan of
the Ages (Col. 1:25-27). **There is a different thrust, a
vital thrust today,** so that the Plan of the Ages should
be fulfilled. This "difference" is discussed more fully in
chapter 6.

Therefore the ministry of Jesus' healing and deliverance
is now being expanded. It is not only to **external** needs
but also to **internal** needs. It is not only to the **obvious**
but to the **hidden**; it is not only to the **isolated** person
in need, here and there, it is to **all** who belong to the
Bride. It is no longer **particular,** but **total.** It has never
been an **option,** but a **command,** for the Lord has commanded, *"Be ye Holy even as I am Holy"* (1 Peter 1:16).
*"You, therefore, must be perfect even as your Heavenly
Father is perfect"* (Matt. 5:48); *cleanse yourselves from
every defilement of flesh and spirit* (2 Cor. 7:1); *be (truly,
fully and continuously) filled with the Spirit* (Eph. 5:18).
Even as John the Baptist preached before the first coming of the Lord, *"Prepare the way of the Lord, make His
paths straight!"*, so today also we must make ourselves
ready (Luke 3:4-9)[1] for the axe of God has truly been
laid at the root of the trees and judgement begins—
indeed has already begun—with the people of God (1
Peter 4:17). The cry goes up again to the people of
God—REPENT! This is not to bring an unclean guilt and
condemnation upon the Church, but it is for her cleansing. Repentance breaks stiff-necked arrogance and
haughtiness, defeats self-justification and pathetic ex-
cuses that constitute self-deception. Repentance enables

[1] See Appendix D.

us to truly forgive others who have sinned against us and therefore, through forgiveness of our own sins, repentance reconciles us totally to our Heavenly Father without any wall of remaining or current sin between us and Him. Repentance breaks the chains which bind us to the leaven of the Pharisees, with which so much of the Bride is bound today!

Thus **the deliverance ministry today is for all who want to be in the Bride of Christ,** and God's Plan will only be achieved by repentance throughout the worldwide church. What a shaking is going to take place—and what a Great Salvation is going to be, and is being, revealed!

But let us heed a warning from the Word of God. In the parable of the Ten (10) Virgins (Matt. 25:1-13) the Lord Jesus teaches us that a large proportion of the Christian Church is going to miss out on the coming of the Bridegroom, due to lukewarmness (not having plenty of oil for their lamps, i.e. not being ready and filled with the Spirit). According to Jesus' teaching the door will be shut—permanently—on (approximately?) 50%—that's right, **HALF** of those who at one time or another had a measure of the oil of the Holy Spirit and were looking for the coming of the Lord.

You might not like the main thrust of this teaching, that a large number of Christians who were once soundly converted—not just nominal unregenerate churchgoers as is commonly supposed—will be shut out from the Wedding Feast in Heaven, but we would be even more foolish than the foolish virgins if we tried to water it down or by any means diminish what God is saying to us through it.

Many people who read this book, some of them well versed in the Scriptures, are going to be highly critical of it—it won't fit into their nicely systematised theology, their understanding of the End-time drama and the deliverance ministry. They are going to voice their objections very strongly, but allowing for my human weakness, no one and no thing is going to persuade me that I am on the wrong track, simply because this course was not invented by me; **I did not choose it nor ask for it but was given it by the irresistible grace of God.** The great ones of the Church denominations can argue till Armageddon comes but by God's grace, NO-ONE is going to rob me of my place amongst the five WISE virgins who were cleansed, full of the Holy Spirit and READY for the Bridegroom—God being my helper. Hallelujah! *HOW ABOUT YOU?*

The Vision again, is:

... **the perfecting of the saints** (believers)
... **to the measure of the stature of the fullness of Christ** (Eph. 4:12-13)
... **through spiritual (inner) cleansing** (James 4:8; 2 Peter 3:13-14)
... **by Deliverance and Restoration programs** (Rom. 12:2; 2 Cor. 7:1)
... **in the Name of the Lord Jesus Christ** (Col. 3:17).

CHAPTER 2

THE PROPHECY OF J. LELAND EARLS

The Vision that we have shared with you is not unique or isolated, but a mighty introduction to it was given to **J. Leland Earls,** the American prophet of the Word of Life Fellowship, Spokane USA, in 1967—before I had attempted to cast out "my" first demon. I have this pastor's permission to quote verbatim from his book **"The Manifested Sons"** Issue No. 3 and trust it will speak to you as loudly and as clearly as it did to me. Words in *ITALICS* are Pastor Leland Earls' emphasis and my added emphasis is in CAPITALS.

God is Moving By His Spirit

"Early in the month of March 1967, the Lord gave me (J. Leland Earls) a prophecy concerning a further moving of His Spirit among those who are being prepared for a great outpouring which is coming. I quote here an excerpt from that prophecy. 'For I say unto you, my people, I am about to move by my Spirit to do a work among my people that they might be prepared to receive a mighty outpouring which is coming. For even this spring of the year 1967 I will begin a new and fresh move among my people to bring about a further development in that spiritual Body which I am raising up. ... I will especially anoint certain vessels of my choosing THAT THEY MAY BE USED TO BRING DELIVERANCE UNTO MY PEOPLE. ESPECIALLY KEEN SHALL BE THE GIFT OF DISCERNMENT, FOR MY PEOPLE HAVE COME UNDER MANY DECEPTIONS AND OPPRESSIONS

OF THE ENEMY, AND THERE IS NEED OF A GREAT CLEANSING AND LIBERATING WORK AMONG MY PEOPLE. Therefore give thyself to me quickly and unreservedly that ye may be used to help cleanse the Body of Christ from all the defilements of the flesh and of the spirit.'

Developments here in the last few days, both in my own experience and in the dealings of the Lord in the local assembly of Christians, indicate to me that this fresh move of the Spirit has already begun. Now we know that the Spirit of God has been moving in a special way for a number of years to call forth and prepare a spiritual Body which is to receive and implement the end-time purposes of God. If you will read carefully the above excerpt from the prophecy you will note that the Lord says His Spirit will begin to move in a new way to bring about a further development in that spiritual Body which He is raising up. In other words it is a fresh impetus to what He is already doing, and among those saints who are OPEN to His moving He will do *a further work of preparation*. THIS PREPARATION, THE PROPHECY SAYS, IS FOR A GREAT OUTPOURING THAT IS COMING. Now just when this great outpouring is coming I do not know.[1] It could be quite near, and it could be several years away. THAT is not important to know right now. But it is important to realise that the Lord is preparing a Body to receive this glorious anointing which is coming. Right now we must move with the Spirit in His work of preparation.

Now notice further that the prophecy says the

---

[1] But WE do, now, praise the Lord!

present move of the Spirit is to BRING A CLEAN-SING AND LIBERATING in the Body of Christ. In order to accomplish this, the Lord says He will especially anoint certain vessels of His choosing, and He will cause the *gift of discernment* to be especially keen among His people. In order to illustrate what God is beginning to do, let me relate an experience which I had on Sunday night, April 16. For several months I have been suffering with an affliction in my body which has made it impossible for me to function as I ought. My internal organs relative to my digestive system have not been working right. I won't go into detail, but as a result of this condition I have been able to do very little ministering. I have had to do most of my writing and typing in bed. After seeking the Lord diligently, I was convinced (confirmed by other mature ministries) that this was yet another symbolic portrayal of the condition of the Body of Christ. This is in harmony with Hosea 12:10 where God says He uses similitudes (patterns) by the ministry of the prophets. Last Sunday evening I began to experience a tremendous burning sensation coming up from my stomach into my throat, accompanied by a bitter taste. As this continued for some time the Lord began to deal with me about the present move of His Spirit and what He purposed to do. He called my attention to Heb. 12:15 where it speaks of the root of bitterness which can defile many. The Lord showed me three kinds of enemy spirits which are especially defiling to members of the Body of Christ today. They are SPIRITS OF JEALOUSY, SPIRITS OF CRITICISM, AND SPIRITS OF RESENTMENT. All three are the fruit of the manifestation of the root of bitterness in people.

Suddenly there flashed before me the crucifixion scene where Jesus was offered vinegar mixed with *gall* (a bitter substance). (See Matt. 27:34). Immediately the words were flashed into my mind: "He refused it." Suddenly my whole system reacted against the burning and bitter sensation which I was experiencing during this period of teaching by the Lord. It was as if supernatural hands took hold of my stomach and internal organs and literally forced me to begin vomiting violently. Up and out went the burning and bitterness. Beloved, *do you get it?* When Jesus went to the Cross to purchase our redemption from all the sins and defilements of the enemy, He refused the gall of bitterness. Symbolically the Lord was enacting the same thing in my body *at the same time the revelation was being flashed to me.* Now we know that Jesus was the pattern for His spiritual Body. Just as Jesus, in His physical body, refused to drink the gall of bitterness, so is that same Jesus, through the discernment and liberating power of His Spirit, going to refuse the spirits of bitterness in His spiritual Body. And these spirits are primarily JEALOUSY, CRITICISM and RESENTMENT.

After this experience the Lord began to deal with me concerning other spirits which are especially troubling the Body of Christ at this time. He showed me two other groups of three each. In the second group are PROUD SPIRITS, RELIGIOUS SPIRITS, AND DECEIVING SPIRITS. In the third group are COVETOUS SPIRITS, LUST SPIRITS, AND LYING SPIRITS.

These six, plus the three "bitter" spirits mentioned

above, are the nine kinds of spirits which are especially defiling the Body of Christ, and ARE
HINDERING THE SAINTS FROM MOVING INTO
THEIR FULL INHERITANCE IN CHRIST. Beloved,
hear me! The present move of the Spirit of God is
primarily to bring cleansing and deliverance from
these spirits of the enemy that the saints be no
longer hindered. I cannot go into all that the Lord
has shown me concerning this subject and the rela-
tion of His present move to it. But I do know that HE
IS RAISING UP AND ANOINTING VESSELS OF
HIS CHOOSING TO BE USED IN THIS MINISTRY.
He has also promised KEEN DISCERNMENT, and
I know that along with this gift will go the GIFTS OF
KNOWLEDGE AND WISDOM, and also MUCH
LOVE AND COMPASSION. FOR THIS IS A MINIS-
TRY OF HELP AND DELIVERANCE, NOT OF
CONDEMNATION. There are many saints who are
vexed and oppressed by one or more of these spir-
its and THEY ARE NOT FULLY AWARE OF IT. THEY
MAY SENSE THAT SOMETHING IS WRONG,
BUT THEY DON'T KNOW WHAT TO DO OR HOW
TO GET DELIVERANCE.

The Lord has shown me that the nine spirits mentioned are the very antithesis of the nine fruits of
the Spirit mentioned in Gal. 5:22-23. How can the
Lord impart love, joy and peace when many saints
are experiencing the bitterness of jealousy, criticism
and resentment. It is impossible for saints to express genuine longsuffering, gentleness and goodness towards others if there are PROUD, RELI-
GIOUS, AND DECEIVING SPIRITS AT WORK IN
THEIR LIVES. There can be very little real fidelity,
meekness and self-control evidenced in those who

have succumbed to covetous, lust and lying spirits. There is so much more that could be written about what the Lord is revealing, but I feel the Spirit would have me draw this to a close.

I feel led to point out one more thing. Notice the inspired statement of Peter in Acts 8:23 as he exposes the jealousy of Simon toward the apostles and his coveting of their power. Peter says, "For I perceive that thou art in the gall of bitterness." These are the two words the Lord kept repeating to me last Sunday evening with reference to my physical condition: "gall" and "bitterness". Then He gave the words "chemical imbalance". Because of this condition in my body, it simply has not been able to function rightly and I have been very limited in what I can do. But now the Lord IS CORRECTING this and my body is beginning to function as it should. Beloved, we cannot expect the spiritual Body of Christ to function in full power and glory until the Spirit has fully liberated it from all the bitter and defiling spirits of the enemy which are so prevalent among the saints today.

I am sure that MOST OF THOSE WHO ARE MOVING ON WITH GOD WOULD LIKE TO AVOID WHAT I HAVE BEEN TALKING ABOUT. But I am convinced there can be no real moving on into the fullness of His Covenant blessings and powers UNTIL THERE HAS BEEN A REAL CLEANSING AND LIBERATING WORK DONE IN HIS SPIRITUAL BODY. And I am also convinced that the Spirit of God is beginning to move in a special way NOW for this type of ministry. Only a special *baptism of His love,* a special *impartation of His wisdom,* and a special *enduement of His anointing* can bring about what He has purposed."[1]

So far we have shared a Vision with you, a Vision that is not isolated but comes to you from ministries in Australia and the U.S.A. and no doubt can be confirmed from many parts of the world, and will be, in God's good time.

Here is the vision yet again. It is so important you get it into your spirit.

> ... **the perfecting of the saints** (believers)
> ... **to the measure of the stature of the fullness of Christ** (Eph. 4:12-13)
> ... **through spiritual (inner) cleansing** (James 4:8; 2 Peter 3:13-14)
> ... **by Deliverance and Restoration programs** (Rom. 12:2; 2 Cor. 7:1)
> ... **in the Name of the Lord Jesus Christ** (Col. 3:17).

It is a Vision that shows us the importance and the place of continuous cleansing by deliverance in the full salvation of Christ for the End-Time, and no doubt you would like to consider the scriptural evidence upon which the Vision is based.

Let us begin to do this.

---

[1] Additional extracts from J. Leland Earls prophecies and others are contained in the Appendices.

CHAPTER 3

THE LORD REVEALS THE HIDDEN PROBLEM—THE MAGNITUDE OF HUMAN DEMONISATION!

Introduction:

WHAT SCRIPTURAL EVIDENCE IS THERE FOR CONTINUOUS CLEANSING (DELIVERANCE AND HEALING)?

I suppose the most common question raised in this matter of continuous ministry is WHY? Why continuous regular cleansing deliverance and healing? Jesus didn't seem to need such methods to obtain the results He did and the Bible seems to be all instant miracles, right? Well, not quite. This question needs quite a deal of answering and that is what this book is all about. There are a number of factors to be considered, so please don't expect a quick thirty-second answer, there isn't one, except to say that WHILE YOU CONTINUE SINNING YOU SHOULD CONTINUE RECEIVING DELIVERANCE MINISTRY. How many days a week do you walk perfectly in the ways of the Lord? Seven days a week? Three days a week? ONE day a week? One hour a week? Well then, I suggest you get into a deliverance program and persevere in what the Lord has commanded (See Appendix D) until you are showing ALL the fruit of the Spirit of God (See Appendix F).

"But," you say, "Aren't you confusing our sinful imperfection with being demonised?" The answer is that I am certainly relating the two together, but we are getting ahead of ourselves here, and as I have said, there is no satisfying quick answer. Let us get back to a step by step evaluation of all the evidence.

To begin, we need to consider the size of the PROBLEM, and consideration of this subject will go a long way towards answering "why continuous cleansing?" **Secondly,** we will need to put under close scrutiny the ministry of Jesus **nineteen centuries ago** and compare it with His ministry through deliverance and healing ministries **today.** When there are significant differences between the two, we ought to note them because where they are valid they will be informative and revelational to us, but most importantly any such comparison should not only be based on experience but also on the Word of God, because the Word of God not only opens up to us the ministry of the Lord Jesus nineteen centuries ago, but it foreshadows the purpose and **nature of His ministry in the End-Time, which is now!**

Perhaps all that confused you a little? Let me summarise that little section another way. The case in support of a CONTINUOUS ministry of deliverance needs to consider, among other things:

(i) The SIZE of the problem of human demonisation as revealed by the Holy Spirit today through the Word of God and our daily Christian experience.

(ii) The ministry of Jesus to the needs of those around Him nineteen centuries ago as revealed in the New Testament.

(iii) The ministry of Jesus TODAY to the needs of this

last generation for His ultimate, concluding purposes in history and the close of the Age, as presented to us in the New Testament.

So what we are saying is we should not expect Jesus' ministry to the demoniacs whom He met during His FIRST coming to be anything more than an INTRODUCTION to what His Word tells us will happen just prior to His SECOND coming. If the Church of God LIMITS the ministry to that of the first apostles how then can the harvest of the LATTER RAIN be brought forth as He desires? But more of this later.

You could feel that while there may be considerable biblical evidence for Jesus' ministry in New Testament days, it will be difficult to find scriptures relating to His ministry today, but in fact **it is all there for us** when we are made aware by the Holy Spirit and know what we are being shown by Him. However, like most answers from God's Word, they are most meaningful to us when we understand the NATURE of the PROBLEM. **If we cannot perceive the problems, how can we receive the answers?** Let us pose our two areas of major concern and revelation again:

(a) What is the magnitude of the problem of human demonisation?

and

(b) How does today's ministry of deliverance by Christ compare with His ministry when on earth nineteen centuries ago?

In examining question (a) above we can divide our study of the extent of human demonisation into three areas or

38

subheadings. They are expressed in statements of fact as follows:

(i)   Large **numbers of spirits** can inhabit humans.

(ii) Huge **numbers of people** need deliverance ministry.

(iii) The **huge complexity** and **variety** of types of spirits.

Let us begin to present the evidence:

(i)   LARGE NUMBERS OF SPIRITS CAN INHABIT HUMANS.

The numbers of individual spirits that can indwell a human being are quite amazing. We know from the unclean spirit called **Legion** (Mark 5:9) that a number between 4000 and 6000—the number of soldiers in a Roman Legion of the day—is not impossible, and yet Legion could speak as ONE spirit, though MANY. You will remember the conversation of Legion with the Lord was full of singular and plural words mixed together, viz:

> "'**My** name is Legion (singular) for **we** are many' (plural). And **he** (Legion) (singular) begged him (Jesus) not to send **them** (plural) out of the country."
>
> (Mark 5:9-10)

We need to remember that ONE unclean spirit reigns over a KINGDOM of lesser unclean spirits and so WE ARE NOT TALKING ABOUT SINGLE INDIVIDUAL SPIRITS, as is commonly thought by Christians, but we are talking about GROUPS OF SPIRITS WHICH MAY

BE PART OF A KINGDOM UNDER A RULING SPIRIT and then again there may be several KINGDOMS IN ONE SOUL making up the TOTAL KINGDOM OR EMPIRE under the rulership of sin and death (Rom. 5:12).

The whole thing is quite revelational and mind-boggling, but the fact remains that satan has a huge empire of RULING, MIDDLE-CLASS and WORKER SPIRITS LIKE SOME VAST, INVISIBLE, CHAOTIC ARMY INSIDE THE SOUL OF EVERY DEMONISED PERSON, and the Lord has given this glimpse into Legion[1] in His Holy Word so that when we experience ongoing conflict with the unclean enemy from within a sufferer, with all his battalions, regiments and divisions drawn up against us in their infinite variety, we shall not be vulnerable to the temptation that WE are departing from Bible truth but we will in fact have a witness from the Holy Spirit to the truth of spiritual warfare at a level not normally perceived in the modern church.

However this knowledge of the large number of spirits which can in fact be called ONE unclean spirit should not deter or discourage us. We know, of course, that Jesus overruled the kingdom (rule) of satan in the man who had the **Legion** with the Kingdom (Rule) of God and we are also told by the Apostle Paul not to let **sin** reign (rule as King) in our mortal bodies (Rom. 6:12,14), so we can conclude that **SIN is a Ruler or kingdom of satan** which attempts to rule the Christian from within, and may add to itself or include other kingdoms such as blindness or dumbness etc.

---

[1] The possibility that the 4000-6000 spirits were RULING class spirits is discussed in Christian Deliverance Book 2 under the sub-heading Counting Numbers of Demons. If they were RULERS, each spirit would probably have at least another hundred under its command.

It is recorded in scripture that **Mary Magdalene** had seven (7) demons cast out of her by Jesus, but if we can perceive from the Legion account that ONE unclean spirit or demon actually represents thousands of spirits of different rank and strength, and that the Bible may count ONE spirit as, in effect, ONE RULING spirit which rules over a kingdom of spirits, then **Mary's plight may have been far worse than we first imagined.**

Is it any wonder that numbers of spirits removed from people who approached me for ministry totalled in the hundreds, sometimes **thousands** PER PERSON! I remember **Pastor Harold Dewberry**[1] ringing up to express surprise at the numbers. "Peter, I understand the type of spirits you are getting" he said, "but I'm amazed at the numbers." I knew that Harold had exercised successful and anointed deliverance ministry, and at the time I wondered why he could get apparently good results so quickly when I had to minister for weeks, even months, to get someone cleaned up.

I didn't **want** to be involved in slow or progressive ministry. I didn't **want** to wade through hundreds of spirits in ONE person one at a time or even ten at a time. It was too exhausting, too never-ending and far too time-consuming. I could think of one hundred different ways of serving the Lord which seemed easier from any angle and far more "fashionable", attractive and acceptable to the rest of the Body of Christ.

I was puzzled why we seemed to be on some kind of deliverance treadmill which seemed to go on forever compared with **Harold's** one-session ministry.

---

[1] Now The Rev. Dr Harold Dewberry.

I asked the Lord why this was so and the clear conviction came to me that **Harold** had a greater anointing for **particular** ministry than I; he could get a group of spirits out in one session and bring a level of significant change to a sufferer's life but I was to be patient and work through continuous ministry because **only in this way could the complex nature and structure of satan's kingdoms within man be exposed, and thus COMPLETELY REMOVED.** What a task, what a thrill! To be one of those called by God to EXPOSE the powers of darkness in mankind prior to the Lord unleashing His full and great salvation across the face of the earth, which must be poured out in order that the Bride should be made ready for the Bridegroom! The inescapable consequence of this revelation is that **the unbelievably large numbers of spirits within people will require a continuous ministry programme** if only for the sake of thoroughness.

So point no. 1 is: **Human beings can have large numbers of unclean spirits dwelling within them, and ONE spirit can mean 6000!**

(ii)   HUGE NUMBERS OF PEOPLE NEED DELIVERANCE MINISTRY

The second thing to amaze me about this ministry was that just about everyone who was tested for an unclean spirit responded positively, i.e. manifested. It would not be wrong to say that we have never been approached by anyone seeking deliverance, who has not NEEDED deliverance.

Just stop for a moment and read that again. Yes, it's true—a 100% need for the application of the deliverance ministry! This was true in my earliest days as well as now. Is it any wonder that **Derek Prince** has gone on record in his tape ministry as saying that 75% of a large congregation responded positively when asked to indicate if they thought they might have need of deliverance. That is three out of four people acknowledging— in public—that they NEEDED deliverance!

Is it any wonder that when a Pentecostal Pastor in New Zealand invited his visiting preacher to minister deliverance, the meeting place was turned into a complete "madhouse" as the whole congregation tried to get into the ministry room? Eventually everybody was told to stay where they were (because the aisles were choked) and apparently the whole congregation received from the Lord right where they were sitting. And noise! The Pastor prayed fervently that the tremendous demonic din would be blotted out by the Lord, and there were no complaints by neighbours that he knew of—praise God!

When we stop to think about it, we should not be surprised. The same powers of darkness that the early church had to contend with are still around today, only they have had eighteen centuries to infiltrate the world and the church with virtually NO OPPOSITION! Even the denominational churches had lost sight of their existence and their method of operation until now. In the past every wrong-doing has been blamed by the church on SIN, the spiritual disease of the human heart, but **we were being taught that the spiritual disease of sin was made up of demons or unclean spirits.** This should not have surprised us, but it did. It was so simple yet so profound and SO un-traditional.

What has happened is that, **through the ministry of**

deliverance, the Lord granted a revelation of the **TRUE SPIRITUAL NATURE OF SIN,** which, in brief, is as follows:—

1. The Bible teaches us that man and woman are created spirit, soul and body (1 Thess. 5:23) and that although the terms "spirit" and "soul" are sometimes used as if they mean the same thing, nevertheless **there is a clear distinction between them** which can be arrived at from studying the Word of God, which is "sharper than any two-edged sword, piercing **to the division of soul and spirit.**" (Hebrews 4:12 RSV).

2. The Bible indicates that **the human soul** (the area of the emotions) **can contain many indwelling spirits in addition to the human spirit** of life (Gen. 2:7; Heb. 12:23), e.g. the man who had the Legion of spirits. When the spirit(s) said to the Lord Jesus "my name is Legion for we are many" (Mark 5:9), it/they did not know how revealing this would be for us today.

In EXTREME cases of multiple personalities (M.P.D.) our secular society normally views such conditions as "emotional instability", schizophrenia or even insanity, but the truth of the matter is the Bible teaches that **EVERYONE is born with spiritual kingdoms of sin and death reigning[1] in their souls,** normally thought of in Christian tradition as "original sin", and when this basic spiritual condition is worsened by continuing enquiry into occult practices, for example, noticeable (public) activity of the spirits of these kingdoms in the soul is not unusual.

---

[1] Sin and death REIGN (as Kings over Kingdoms) in the hearts of mankind (Romans 5:12, 14, 21).

44

3. In addition, when we become a Christian we receive the **Holy Spirit (of Christ)** into our souls (Rom. 8:9) so that our **human spirit** which was dead (drowning) in trespasses and sin (Eph. 2:2) is born again (or anew, or from above). Our dead spirit is made alive by the Spirit of the Lord Jesus and we are transferred from the kingdom of darkness into the Kingdom of God (Col. 1:13-14). The indwelling Holy Spirit is our seal and guarantee that we belong to God (2 Cor. 1:21-22) and He not only revives the human spirit but helps us to wage war against all that is unclean in the soul as well. Praise the Lord!

4. The Bible teaches that everyone is a sinner (Rom. 3:23) and has **a deposit of sin and death** transmitted down to them from generation to generation (Rom. 5:12; 1 John 1:8). The Bible also teaches that **the transmitted disease of original sin is inspired by an unclean spirit** (Eph. 2:2; Matt. 12:33-45)[1] within the human soul and is referred to as the **strong man,** the **old man** or **old nature,** because it strives to rule over the human spirit—before—**and after**—we are converted to Christ.

The very first reference to sin in the scriptures, when the subject is introduced, personalises sin. Sin is not some nebulous, airy-fairy, abstract "it" but a "he" and I believe the **New American Bible—Catholic Edition—** gives us the best translation:—

God speaks to Cain: "If you do well you can hold up your head, but if not, **sin is a demon** lurking at the door; **his** urge is towards you, yet you can be **his** master" (Gen. 4:7).

---

[1] Discussed more fully in Christian Deliverance Book 4 "Discerning Human Nature".

The footnote of this translation tells us that the words **"demon lurking"** are translated from the literal "crouches" and allude to the similar **Akkadian**[1] term to designate **a certain kind of evil spirit.**

Perhaps you may find this literal translation a revelational shock to your thinking and suspect the **Roman Catholic** translators of some inaccuracy but let me assure you they are not the only ones who have perceived this revelation that **SIN is a living personality,** and a **demonic personality** at that. I offer you five supporting pieces of testimony:

(i)   **"The Analytical Hebrew and Chaldee Lexicon"** (p. 674) lists the Hebrew word for "crouching" or "lurking" as an active singular MASCULINE participle and therefore warrants references to SIN as a HE or HIS (N.A.B.-Catholic Ed.) and HIS and HIM (R.V.) etc. rather than an IT.

(ii) Also the same lexicon (p. 779) indicates that the Hebrew noun for "desire" has a masculine suffix, warranting the translation "HIS desire" rather than "ITS desire". Furthermore the Hebrew word for the phrase "over it" has a masculine suffix (p. 70). This warrants the last part of Genesis 4:7 being translated as "and you shall rule over **him**".

(iii) The **New International Version** of the Bible is also very supportive of the N.A.B. version but the translators here were not quite bold enough to put the literal translation into the text, but did the next best thing. In the Study version of this Bible translation

---

[1] Semitic language of Akkad in ancient Babylonia.

of Genesis 4:7 they put in a vital explanatory footnote:

> *"4:7 **sin is crouching at your door.** The Hebrew word for "crouching" is the same as an ancient Babylonian word referring to an evil demon crouching at the door of a building to threaten the people inside. **Sin may thus be pictured here as just such a demon,** waiting to pounce on Cain—it desires to have him. He may already have been plotting his brother's murder."*

The only comment I wish to make on this footnote is to say that **sin IS to be seen and understood as a demon,** not simply MAY be so pictured. That seems to be the plain meaning of the text.

(iv) The most powerful support for the N.A.B. translation that "SIN IS A DEMON lurking ..." comes from the Lord Jesus Christ Himself. In Matthew Chapter 12, verses 38 to 45, the Lord explains something of the unclean inspiration behind the evil and adulterous generation that craves a sign. Once we understand that sin is a demon which was crouching at the door of Cain's body and soul, and that his response to God's warning would dictate whether or not the demon could enter Cain to "possess" him, that is, his (Cain's) house, we can immediately see that Jesus was alluding to the Genesis passage and its revelation of the operation of the sin demon upon, outside and within a man's house (body). This is what the Lord Jesus actually said:

> *43: "Now **when the unclean spirit goes out from a man,** he goes through dry places seeking rest and does not find (any).*

*44: **Then he says 'I will return into my house** from which I came out'. And when he comes he finds it standing empty, swept and furnished (ready for occupancy).*

*45: Then he goes and takes with himself seven other spirits more evil than himself, and **they enter and dwell there; and the last state of that man** becomes worse than the first. **So it will be also with this evil generation.**"* (Matt. 12:43-45 lit. with added words in parenthesis).

(v) It is about time we began to believe some of the descriptions of the Word of God about our inner-most pollution.

The **apostle Paul** repeatedly refers to our **Old Man** (Rom. 6:6, Eph. 4:22, Col. 3:9) which is corrupt, while the Lord Jesus refers to the **Strong (man)** who rules his "house" (Matt. 12:29). Neither should we lose sight of the **satanised Peter** whom the Lord rebuked with:

*"**Get behind me, satan! You are an offence (stumbling block) to me, because you do not think the way God thinks, but the way men think (Matt. 16:23).***

You can see from this that **the natural minds of men are spiritually polluted and satanised** (cf. James 3:15). They don't have a clue about God's mind even though they are surrounded by the witness of His creation, because their minds and hearts have become darkened (Rom. 1:18-22). **It is only through the Word of God, made alive by the Spirit of God, that mankind can**

begin to understand the truth of the mind of God.
(Isaiah 55:8-11; John 6:63, 8:31-32, 14:6, 17:17; 1 Cor.
2:10-16; 2 Cor. 3:6; Eph. 1:17-18).

Two questions for you:

(a)   Do you believe Jesus' teaching?

(b)   Can you see that in referring to a man as a
house with a demon or unclean spirit lurking
outside, looking for a suitable place (house)
to rest or dwell in, **Jesus was referring to
and expanding the literal meaning of Genesis 4:7**, where sin is a demon lurking at the
door of Cain's body and soul?

It should not surprise us that the Bible says everyone
who has a root of sin in their heart has unclean spirits,
because the church has always (to my knowledge) defined "sin" as **the spiritual disease of the human heart.**
Now, "spiritual" is further defined as "of the spirit", that
is, **sin IS spiritual,** which must obviously mean inspired
by spirits or a spirit. It is really so simple. It seems incredible the church could overlook that **spiritual things
(problems) are caused by spirits** all these centuries—
especially the spiritual nature of the human heart.

**Therefore every SINNER has a SPIRITUAL problem;
that is the teaching of the Bible,** but what about practical experience?

When people suggest that I am demon-happy and find
demons under every stone, I can only answer that we
are prepared to test anyone for demonisation in order
to find out the truth. One cannot get a demon out of

somebody if it isn't there in the first place, any more than one can get blood out of a stone. The "trouble" is that the tests are ALWAYS positive. That may not be pleasing news to you but it is true and must be faced, for no amount of theological wriggling can get around it. The test sample has been quite large—over a thousand sufferers,[1] and continues to increase.

So point no. 2 is: **A very large number of Christian people are prepared to admit to the truth that the Bible says they need deliverance. Indeed EVERY SIN-NER, Christian or otherwise, NEEDS DELIVERANCE.**

(iii) THE HUGE COMPLEXITY AND VARIETY OF TYPES OF SPIRITS.

What is the difference between sins caused by SIN, and sins caused by demons? **NONE, if what we have just said the Bible says is true,** and if our experience is any guide, because you can name almost any sin you can think of, and I can testify that we have ministered against unclean spirits of that name. **There isn't any sin that doesn't have a matching unclean spirit!** Likewise for sickness and it seems likewise for poisons also. Incredible as it may seem, we have ministered against spirits of mercury poisoning and radium poisoning/destruction, against abortion spirits and I even had spirits of **navigational confusion** ministered out of myself. I always had a poor sense of direction and could never find my way around our city and suburban roads without frequent references to the road-map. If there was a wrong choice to make, I would make it—until I received ministry for this problem.

---

[1] Up to 1989

When you stop to think about it, we should all have the same abilities. We all come from Adam and Eve, and therefore should each have the same capacity for the same things, as **God created human beings perfect— before the Fall.**

If we were made perfect BEFORE man's Fall from grace, and if, as we Christians believe, this Fall from grace is responsible for the less-than-perfect state of mankind today, it follows that our so-called physical gifts, or lack of them, are not so much what God has given us as a kind of bonus, but rather what God has NOT PERMITTED satan to take away from us.

To put it another way, it is not so much that God has given some of us special physical gifts to use, which He has withheld from others (e.g. a good memory), but rather that He has given us all, through the creation of Adam (before the Fall), the same physical, natural gifts, only the "normal" 100% has been blocked off or curtailed or reduced by, for example mind-binding spirits, or some other unclean, defiling or disfiguring agencies which express the deposit of sin and death within us all, and which prevent us from utilising our God-given 100% ability.

God gave Adam **everything** (before the Fall) except the knowledge of evil, and **satan is the one who has robbed us.** When the deliverance ministry of Christ takes "captivity captive" (Eph. 4:8) we find we have a POTENTIAL we never thought possible regarding the basic gifts of creation or nature, quite apart from the supernatural gifts of the Spirit.

It is not that the mathematician has a special gift

**from God but rather that the person who struggles
with "maths" has been robbed by satan.** My terrible
sense of direction (before being delivered) was not God's
doing, but satan's. My wife could never sing in tune. It
had been a standing joke in our family for 25 years.
Before I met her she once tried to join the church choir
but without success and we all thought that one either
has a voice or one hasn't—singing voices are a gift
from God. But we were wrong. As Verlie draws closer to
Jesus and following on her own cleansing by deliverance, and growing ministry to others, to her great de-
light she is finding that she can sing in tune (sometimes!) and to my utter amazement the Lord has made
a song (worship) leader out of her. As satan's defiling,
distorting hand on her life is being reduced her **original
creation abilities are re-emerging! "For God made
all things well!"** (Gen. 1:10, 12, 18, 21, 25, 31). Hallelujah!

But I can hear some of you saying within your spirit
"Now hold on for a moment Peter, what you have said
would mean that there are an enormous variety of spirits in the world because they are responsible (in the
spirit realm) for all of mankind's failings, i.e. lack of perfection?"

That's right!

"But I don't see this kind of evidence in the Bible." Well,
it is all there. The Scriptures tell us that a matter is
established at the mouth of two or three witnesses (Deut.
19:15) and we are more than able to find sufficient testimonies from both the Old and the New Testaments.
First let us look at FIVE (5) areas where unclean spirits
are clearly responsible for human bondage!

1. Osteogenic affliction

The "daughter of Abraham" with the curvature of the spine is described as being bound by satan and having a **spirit of Infirmity.** Once it is conceded that satan is responsible for sickness it would seem to be intellectually indefensible to deny the activity of an unclean spirit (Luke 13:10-16).

2. Physical affliction of sense organs

The **dumb** and **deaf** lad (Mark 9:25)
The **blind** and **dumb** demoniac (Matt. 12:22-24)
These are PHYSICAL afflictions caused by spirits.

3. Mental and emotional disturbance

Legion is generally considered the most extreme case in the scriptures and we know from a synopsis of the New Testament evidence that he was **violent** and **suicidal,** motivated by powerful and destructive forces. **Psychotic,** perhaps even homicidal, he was beyond human help and only the ministry of Christ could free him (Mark 5:1-20). We ask you to consider this case again a little further on.

4. Debilitating mind disorder

The dumb and deaf lad was apparently also **epileptic** and took destructive fits (Matt. 17:15-18, Luke 9:39).

5. Occult bondage

The slave girl with a spirit of **divination** (a python)

is the key incident. Notice that the occult inspiration speaks the truth and is therefore very deceptive but its unclean nature is revealed by its effect of hindering the proclamation of God's Word. There is no request for help from the girl but the incident reveals a sharp conflict between the unclean spirit and the Holy Spirit. The unclean is no match. (Acts 16:16-18).

Dear Brethren, we do not have to put up with an unclean spirit hindering us preaching the Word of God!

But it is not only the more obvious forms of bondage with which we are concerned, such as blindness and dumbness, but with the whole range of human frailties such as anger, condemnation, rejection etc. I remember a young married couple coming to me after having come to our meetings for several months and the young man was unhappy with his spiritual condition. "Peter", he said, "I don't seem to be making any progress—I don't feel very good at all—what's wrong?" So I dug out of my confidential file the personal details of his life which he had given me when he first came to us for help. "Well", I asked, "have you still got that terrible jealousy when your wife talks to another man?" "No", he said, "that seems to have gone." "Have you still got that violent streak in you that causes you to strike her?" "No" he said, looking a little brighter, "I haven't hit her for ages." "Do you still get angry with her?" "No." He was beginning to look positively cheerful at this point. "Hey, I'm glad I came and talked to you. I didn't realise how much progress I had made!" We went through another half dozen spiritual problems of which the young man had complained when he first came to us and they had all virtually disappeared BUT the Holy Spirit had continued to search him out in the innermost parts of his being, and **NOW he was manifesting a whole new range of problems which he didn't even know he had.**

If we had not been able to compare his earlier condition (from our records) with his present experience, the evil one would have been able to convince him that the ministry was no good, he was wasting his time and in fact he was (felt) worse, not better. He would have left the ministry and taken away with him a miserable testimony which satan would have been able to use to discourage others, and the Lord would have received no thanksgiving or glory, which is His due.

I share his account with you because it is not an uncommon situation and recurs regularly. It not only underlines some of the enemy's battle tactics which have deceived many in the past (and unfortunately will endeavour to do so in the future) but it illustrates the truth that **there is a WIDE RANGE of spiritual problems in the children of God,** most of whom are almost completely unaware of the full, true situation within them.

I am often asked on what scriptural authority do I base my views that human personality difficulties such as fear, resentment, guilt, terror, depression, frustration, anger, murder, destruction, lying, deceit, sorrow, etc. etc. may be caused by the activity of unclean spirits, when the scriptures do not give detailed information. The answer is that there is plenty of evidence in the scriptures, if you are prepared to take the trouble to look for it. **In addition to the five areas** from the New Testament already listed we can add the following spirits:

Bondage to fear	Romans 8:15
Fear/timidity	2 Tim. 1:7
Stupor/stupefaction	Romans 11:8
Antichrist	1 John 4:3
Error	1 John 4:6

and from the Old Testament spirits of:

Jealousy	Numbers 5:14 cf. Acts 5:17
Lying	1 Kings 22:19-23
Pride	Eccles. 7:8
Harlotry	Hosea 4:12, 5:4

When we add these to the five areas already presented we certainly have a wide range of references.

The point is that once the spiritual warfare between Christ and satan is clearly defined there are enough examples such as we have listed to establish links between immoral, ugly or destructive human behaviour and demons. The scriptures only require the evidence of two or three testimonies to establish a matter and therefore do not give us a detailed list of antichrist's activities simply because the list would be endless, while outward forms of attack, especially those of an occult character (e.g. eastern mysticism) may change from age to age. It is sufficient for the Word of God to give us the principles, to be applied by Christian soldiers with discernment in the age in which they live.

Talking about Christian soldiers with discernment, have you ever closely considered the case of the man with the **Legion?** Just take a minute to look at the biblical evidence:

1. He didn't live in houses like   Luke 8:27-29
   other people, but in the tombs   Mark 5:3
   (unclean to Jews)

2. He ran around naked   Luke 8:27

3. The spirits in him were quite
   happy to transfer into swine   Mark 5:12
   (unclean to Jews)

4. He was very fierce and very,   Matt 8:28
   very strong   Mark 5:3

5. He often cried out with a
   loud voice   Mark 5:5-7

6. He cut himself with stones   Mark 5:5-7
                                           (cf. 1Kings 18:28)

7. After his deliverance he is
   described as being "in his   Mark 5:15
   right mind"

Do you have any discernment on the complex range and variety of spirits that made up the kingdoms of darkness ruled over by "Legion"?[1] Whether you do or whether you don't, I believe I have made point no. 3, that is, **there is a huge complexity and variety of types of spirits plaguing mankind, a range as wide as sin itself, for wherever there is a sin to name, there is a demon to match it, indeed to inspire it!**

In my view it should not be too much to ask of a Christian

---

[1] Discussed briefly in Christian Deliverance Book 2 "Engaging the Enemy", Chap. 5. 3.

that when he repents daily for his sins, he recognizes demons, acting upon his old nature (that is, his flesh wherein sin dwells—Romans 7), have led him astray; because it can be demonstrated from the scriptures that **demons cause sin, false worship** and **false teaching** among other things. Therefore it is not horrible, disgraceful or insulting for a Pastor to say that someone is affected by demons. He is simply telling a truth that applies to every sinner[1] (Eph. 6:12 etc.), and facing the truth without fuss is essential if the enemy is to be put to flight. As the Bible teaches that EVERY sinner is affected by demons, the question of DEGREE becomes very important.

So what have we said in this chapter? We have endeavoured to establish that:

1.   **Large numbers of spirits can inhabit humans**
2.   **Huge numbers of people (everyone?) need deliverance ministry**
3.   **There Is a huge variety of types of spirits.**

All of which confirms the magnitude of the PROBLEM, that is, the magnitude of HUMAN DEMONISATION, which I trust has now been established beyond doubt for those who believe the Bible.

(iv) EZEKIEL'S WARNING

I realise that what has been said in this chapter may be unpalatable to many pastors and ministers. Because they are responsible to God for the spiritual well-being and protection of their flock and because MOST Pastors,

---

[1] Discussed more fully in Book 4 "Discerning Human Nature".

the vast majority, CARE about the sheep entrusted to them, I urge each one to solemnly consider the warnings of the Lord to false shepherds contained in Ezekiel Chapter 34.

I sat in an alive church for two years after I had myself received extensive deliverance ministry, and as the Holy Spirit ministered to me over that period I began to receive discerning of spirits on people worshipping the Lord all around where I was sitting. As the months went by I received more and more discernment. I began to minister deliverance to a small number of people at the Pastor's request and soon other people were coming directly to me, to ask if I would minister to them. These sufferers I always referred back to the Pastor to get his permission before proceeding. But then the referrals and the "permissions given" dried up. People in desperate need, whom I had referred to the Pastor, were not being sent back. Then one day a drug-damaged young man asked one Pastor, with whom I was conversing, for help and I was invited to sit in on the counselling. The poor lad was distressed and confused and obviously suffering from a measure of brain damage. He pleaded for help in Christ's Name. The Pastor said what Pastors all over the world say, that Christ was the answer, get into the Word of God, praise the Lord and keep your spiritual eyes focussed on the Cross of Calvary etc. etc. He then dismissed the lad, who had brightened up considerably during the Pastor's encouraging counselling, and asked me what I thought. I agreed with everything he had said, then added that he needed considerable deliverance ministry and mentioned five or six different unclean kingdoms of spirits which had bound the lad in "chains". Nothing more happened and I began to realise **that the gift of discernment separates one from other**

Christians, unless they COMPLETELY trust you. You become a king-size problem and a challenge to them. I really expected the lad to be referred to me within a couple of weeks, if not immediately, but when nothing happened my soul was filled with the grief of God's Spirit to think that young man would continue to suffer, without the kind of help he really needed. His counselling had not been wrong—simply inadequate. He had received a temporary lift in his spirit, but because of the enormous spiritual chains with which he had been bound, his problems had not been removed but simply disarmed for a brief hour—rather like putting a large band-aid on an amputation.

As the weeks went by I began to be continually grieved in my spirit in church. There were so many praising God, singing "I'm free", but still in chains and unaware of it. I began to know a great burden, and going to church where I was surrounded by needy Christians made the burden far worse.

I went to another church. Again the same clapping, praising and ministry of encouragement, but again the same burden as I perceived the bonds of my brothers and sisters in Christ. And again, the discerning of spirits that I was receiving from the Lord was not shared or accepted by those in leadership. The Holy Spirit finally convicted me that THERE WAS NO LOCAL MINISTER UNDER WHOSE AUTHORITY I COULD WORK THIS WORK. They did not see what I could see and did not understand what I now understood and therefore **could not support the ministry that I now knew to be necessary for God's people.** I had referred several heavily-demonised, sad cases to their pastors, expecting to get approval to proceed with their deliverance, without

60

success. These afflicted people continued to carry an ongoing, hourly burden, when I knew that Christ had suffered and died to set them free, but they were DE-NIED the deliverance of Christ by blind shepherds who tell them, "You don't need deliverance—all you need is love." When I heard of this the fire of God burned within my soul and I resolved never again by God's grace would I concern myself with the permission of men whose ideas of God's love are blinkered.

Even now I feel remorse at not ministering to those who asked me for help and whom I then referred on; I know what I did was right in theory and justifiable in con-science as I myself was under authority, but the end result was disastrous.

Today, while we obviously would prefer to have the co-operation and support of the shepherd concerned, we minister on the same basis as Christ and the apostles, that is, WHEN ASKED, AND AS NEEDED, WITHOUT checking with the Chief Priests, scribes and the rulers of the synagogues. If the religionists don't like it, what is new about that? Any TRUE shepherd would be glad to have sheep released from bondage and if they are more concerned about ministry jealousy and their own status, clerical "ethics" and "rights", than they are about the well-being of their people, then they are not a true shep-herd and should ponder the warning of **Ezekiel:**

"The weak you have not strengthened, the sick you have not healed, the crippled you have not bound up, the strayed you have not sought, and with force and harshness you have ruled them ... therefore, you shepherds, hear the word of the LORD. Thus says the Lord GOD, behold,

I am against the shepherds; and I will require my sheep at their hand, and put a stop to their feeding the sheep; no longer shall the shepherds feed themselves. I will rescue my sheep from their mouths, that they may not be food for them. For thus says the Lord GOD: Behold, I, I myself will search for my sheep, and will seek them out.[1] As a shepherd seeks out his flock when some of his sheep have been scattered abroad, so will I seek out my sheep, and I will rescue them from all places where they have been scattered on a day of clouds and thick darkness."

(Ezekiel 34: 4, 9-12 R.S.V.)

God being our helper, never again will we withhold ministry from any man, woman, boy or girl because of the fears, jealousies, whims, opinions or misunderstandings of men. Praise the Name of the Lord!

---

[1] Consider the sovereign move of the Holy Spirit today, across the world—sometimes called the "Toronto Blessing."

CHAPTER 4

CONTINUOUS DELIVERANCE

(i) GOD'S UNFOLDING PLAN

When we consider the Bible, our understanding of it must take into account the evidence of the context, such as who is speaking, who is spoken to, what are the surrounding circumstances of the day, the application of those circumstances to today and whether there has been any further or later revelation in the Scriptures. Is the information ethical, prophetic or doctrinal etc., etc.? One area of biblical debate centres on whether God has completed His revelation to mankind with the Bible or whether His revelation of Himself and His kingdom is a progressive thing, with our knowledge of God being added to in each century? Well, of course, this latter question is not an "either—or" situation, for **both propositions are true.** God has given a "complete" revelation of Himself in the Bible for His creatures and the scriptures should not be added to by other so-called scriptures. However it is also true that God's revelation is progressive in the sense that His Holy Spirit opens up the Word of God from age to age, in order to reveal more of our King and His Kingdom. Thus down through history an outpouring of the Holy Spirit brings fresh truth to the Church of God. **It is OLD TRUTH FROM THE BIBLE, BUT NEW TO THE CHURCH as the Spirit unfolds the knowledge of God progressively from the Word, enabling God's plan of TOTAL RESTORATION for mankind to advance according to His time-table.**

64

What we need to consider, when we are measuring or comparing what the Lord is doing today with what was done in Bible days, is **where do we stand now in the timing of God's unfolding will?** (And this presupposes that our understanding of the events of Jesus' earthly walk was 100% correct in the first place, which of course, no one could substantiate). To compare ministry today, with Jesus' earthly ministry then, without taking into account Jesus' prophetic ministry about the FUTURE of the Kingdom He was sent to establish, is altogether too misguided and inadequate. Spiritual principles do not change, it is true, but we have been warned that the Heavens and the earth will be shaken and what God has said about the End-Time and the cleansing of the Bride does not change either, but is UNFOLDED, STEP BY STEP to a seeing and a listening church. The big question is, do we have eyes to see and ears to hear and hearts to perceive...?

(ii) THE OLD TESTAMENT

The deliverance ministry has often been compared to the Children of Israel's invasion of the Promised Land. Sometimes it appears there are giants in the Land (Numbers 13:30f) and the faint-hearted are afraid to tackle the enemy because they do not really believe God's Word that they are able to go in and possess it because it is given to them (Numbers 13:2, Josh. 1:3). Even though the Land was given to them by the promise of God, i.e. the AUTHORITY of God, they still had to go in and claim it; fight for it with the POWER of God if necessary (Deut. 7:16-18). It is therefore interesting to note that Moses goes on to say: *"And the Lord your God will cast out those nations before you little by little; you may not consume them at once lest the beasts of the field increase upon you"* (Deut. 7:22f; Exod. 23:29-33). Here is an amazing explanation for the GRADUAL entry into victory by the Hebrews against their enemies. **The enemy were to be dispossessed "little by little"** and this would work to the benefit of God's people. So it is with casting out demons today.

It is a fact of life that victories we have to fight for are cherished, and ground won in battle is held jealously and tenaciously. Thus our Christian armour should always be "on" so that every counter-attack to devour us (like beasts of the field) comes to nothing. Indeed, there are many similarities between the warfare conducted by Joshua in the Old Testament and the warfare conducted by Jesus and His apostles in the New Testament, as can be seen in our comparison table (next page).

(iii) THE NEW TESTAMENT

This continuous ministry (warfare) principle is carried on into the New Covenant, more than most of us realise.

Quick and easy victories produce smugness and carelessness which result in our eventual undoing. This is so important I would like you to re-read that again slowly. QUICK AND EASY VICTORIES produce smugness and carelessness which result in our eventual undoing. To illustrate this let us examine the incident where Jesus healed ten (10) lepers (Luke 17:11-19). The details of the story are that ten lepers cried out to Jesus to have mercy on them and He directed them to go and show themselves to the priests, because it was an Old Testament law that they should be declared clean by a priest before Israel could accept them back into normal community life.

66

The lepers exercised faith in the word that Jesus spoke to them so that *"as they went they were CLEANSED".* Then one of them, when he saw that he was CURED, turned back, praising God with a loud voice: and he fell on his face at Jesus' feet, giving Him thanks. Now he was a Samaritan (i.e. a despised half-caste). Then said Jesus *"Were not ten cleansed? Where are the nine? Was no one found to return and give praise to God except this outsider (foreigner)?"* And He said to him, *"Rise and go your way; your faith has SAVED you."*

The first thing to note is that if NINE lepers out of TEN lepers take a speedy and apparently easily received healing somewhat for granted so that they forgot to praise, thank and worship the Son of God who healed them, we should not be surprised that many speedy healings today do not seem to teach some of us much about gratitude to the God who made us well.

Just think for a moment, before we get too critical of the nine ungrateful lepers, because they really do represent a significant portion of the Body of Christ. How many times I have beseeched the Lord over an important matter and when my prayer was answered I breathed a sigh of relief and said "Praise the Lord" automatically and then forgot all about the victory as I became embroiled in more spiritual battles.

Often I have been pulled up by the Holy Spirit some hours later, who has convicted me that my brief and automatic praise was not acceptable to Him because my fleshly relief had robbed me of genuine sincerity. Just as our earthly fathers appreciate gratitude when they are good to us so also the Lord wants us to thank Him from our hearts and spirits, when He is good to us. He certainly does not appreciate being taken for granted.

COMPARISON OF SPIRITUAL WARFARE

OLD TESTAMENT WARFARE	DELIVERANCE TODAY
1. The Lord's leader is named Joshua	Same—The Lord's leader is named Jesus (which is Joshua in Hebrew)
2. The Word of God says—it's yours—go in and take it (Deut. 2:24, Josh. 1:1-9)	The Word of God says—"I give you authority—over all the power of the enemy." (Luke 10:19, Matt. 28:18-20)
3. But the victory has to be claimed and won (Deut. 2:24)	Same—(Luke 10:17)
4. **Unclean kingdoms of flesh are driven out (Deut. 2:36, Josh. 23:9-10)**	**Unclean kingdoms of spirits are driven out (Matt. 12:24-28)**
5. There may be some failures (Josh. 15:63, 16:10, 17:12-13)	Same—see Chapter 9, Book 3 (Mark 9:28)
6. Making deals with the enemy causes problems (Josh. 9, 23: 12-13)	Same—see Chapter 1, subheading "Exorcism", Book 1
7. The enemy tries deception in order to stay put (Josh. 9)	Same—compare the occult woman with the spirit of a python (Acts 16:16-18)
8. Gradual victories work out for the best. Speedy victories make us vulnerable to further attacks (Deut. 7:22).	Same—study this chapter carefully and compare Deut. 7 and the ten lepers (Luke 17:11-19), nine of whom were ungrateful.

If indeed it is true that the PHYSICAL battles engaged in by Joshua and the Jews to enter Canaan and overcome its inhabitants are types or forerunners of the SPIRITUAL battles we read of in the New Testament, and experience today in deliverance work, and I do not doubt that, then this is solid evidence for continuous deliverance today obtaining gradual results—battle by battle—until the war is won in our souls and we are truly filled with the Holy Spirit continuously.

Does this situation seem familiar to you too? If so it will not surprise you that many Christians experience quick healings and deliverances and STILL back-slide because of the self-will that remains in their hearts.

Secondly, we can learn from the distinction Jesus makes between the NINE who were CLEANSED and CURED (literally "doctored") and the Samaritan who was cleansed, cured and SAVED. The word SAVED is very broad and covers all forms of salvation from danger and I believe that the Samaritan, **by the attitude of his heart,** would be a sharer in the FULL SALVATION of God and no doubt numbered amongst the early converts of the Church after Pentecost. As for the others? Well, that would depend on their attitude to Jesus from the time of the Crucifixion onwards. Their miraculous healing was in itself no guarantee that they would later respond to the gospel with the necessary "repentant heart" attitude; that is, **they MAY have been grateful for their healing but not prepared to change the direction of their lives towards God.**

So the biblical evidence seems to point to the fact that quick and easily obtained victories do not necessarily evoke in us the right attitudes to God, and for this rea-son—FOR OUR OWN GOOD—He delivers us LITTLE BY LITTLE. After a deliverance meeting very few of us are in the position where we can withdraw from the world and be nursed in private, free from all worldly pressures. We have families to feed—household chores—jobs to keep and many and various responsibilities to other people. We **also have to adjust to the many changes taking place within us.** All of this is not easy. We dis-cover that we do not know what we are really like and we can become unsettled and confused if we lose sight of our aims in Christ and Who is In control. We would indeed **become easy prey for the spiritual beasts of this world,** and if we are not strengthened in Christ by His Spirit as we are cleansed then, of course, the "seven times worse" state may become a reality.

Dr. Paul Yonggi Cho recounted a similar experience of discovery when speaking at a Convention in Sydney during 1982. He told how he was casting out a spirit of **epilepsy** and it was necessary to persist with exercising his authority in Jesus Christ for three (3) hours before the unclean spirit would leave. He said:–

> "You know usually satan would resist you INCH BY INCH. When I came out of Bible School I had the idea that satan would FLEE easily, like that ... but through my experience (I learned that) satan was fighting INCH by INCH."

> "Come out in Jesus' Name!"

> "No, we are not coming out—why should we..."

The unclean spirits put up every kind of resistance but Dr. Cho persisted through to victory.

There are a number of possible instances of progressive healings and deliverances in the New Testament. For example:

Eutychus (Acts 20:9-12)—fell out of a window while listening to the apostle Paul. He was apparently dead but after Paul embraced him (in the manner of the Old Testament prophets—1 Kings 17:21-22; 2 Kings 4:32-35) he was able to testify that "his soul is in him." Both the Elijah and Elisha incidents recorded in Kings illustrate determined, continuous ministry.

The Blind Man (Mark 8:22-26). This is a classic and obvious case which testifies to the need of a second touch for some situations. If the Lord Jesus Christ who, during His earthly walk, was anointed with the oil of gladness more than His fellows (Hebrews 1:9), needed to minister more power with a second touch, how much more are we, with our lesser anointing and little power (Rev. 3:8), required to maintain our ministry wherever necessary until victory is manifested!

The Syrophonecian Woman (Mark 7:24-30)—has to be very persistent before the barriers to the deliverance of her daughter are swept aside by the Lord. She overcomes His irritated disciples with her pestering (Matt. 15:23) and then two points of order put to her by the Lord (Matt. 15:24-27).

Paul's Thorn in the Flesh (2 Cor. 12:7-10). It may surprise you to read about this subject here because most of the discussion about Paul's thorn has centred on whether or not it was a sickness. On that fact is supposed to hang the case as to whether or not we Christians should believe it is God's perfect will to heal ALL sickness.

If we can assume (and it is a very big IF) for the purposes of our discussion that weakness and weaknesses (v. 9-10) should be translated "sickness" and that Paul asked the Lord three times for healing (v. 8) it amazes me that almost everyone should take the view that the Lord's answer was "No"! The answer was not "No", it was *"My grace is sufficient for you."* That is neither a

YES nor a NO answer. What are the other possibilities (apart from meaning "No")?

(i) It is a **"Wait on the Lord"** type answer and no doubt it would apply until such time as the "abundance of revelations" ceased to be a threat to Paul's ministry by means of puffing him up with pride.

(ii) It is God's way of saying to Paul "You do it! Believe my Word for yourself! You have all the authority and power you need. Don't tell me the problem any more. I know it. **(You) use the authority I have given you and take the victory."** (Luke 10:19 cf. Moses— Exod. 14:15-16).

(iii) It is God's way of saying to Paul, **"You are being healed (progressively).** Hold the faith position regarding my promises of healing and deliverance and the battle my Son won on the Cross will soon be experienced in your flesh."

I suggest that the "no" answer is far and away the weakest possible interpretation of the passage and that any of the other interpretations, or a combination of them, is closer to the Lord's meaning. So, I put it to you that even if we assume that Paul's thorn was an infirmity, the text only shows that not all healings come quickly and easily, especially if there is a lesson to learn.

Trophimus (2 Tim. 4:20)—WAS LEFT SICK at Miletus by Paul. Was he healed or wasn't he? I believe YES, in God's TIME, which brings us to a very interesting subject in the next chapter.

Only recently a brother whose wife was receiving deliverance from **Hindu spirits** became puzzled. His early attempts to minister to his wife had been blessed with success but now he had struck problems. "They are stubborn" he said with an incredulous tone in his voice. "They keep saying 'No, no, no' and won't come out". He was discovering the fallacy of easy victories and why we as a ministry conduct deliverance in our **group meetings where there is Praise, and the Word of God and the POWER of God.** That way there is no respite for the demons from beginning to end. Their stubbornness is broken down as a hammer breaks rock into pieces (Jer. 23:29), for there is no respite for them—from hour to hour, day to day, meeting to meeting and month to month. The ministry is applied by the Spirit, as and when He sees fit, relentlessly, thoroughly, compassionately and continuously. How else shall the children of God be purged from **every** weight of flesh and spirit? (2 Cor. 7:1).

SUMMARY

I trust we have been able to show that continuous warfare is really nothing new for the people of God in Old Testament or New Testament times, although the concept of regular weekly Deliverance and Restoration meetings for inner cleansing and purifying is obviously an End-Time leading and thrust of the Holy Spirit.

However continuous deliverance ministry is only part of the total package. If the people of God are to fulfil God's perfect, predestined plan for each one of them, that they be fully conformed to the image of the Son of God (Rom. 8:29), they will need more than ISOLATED deliverance ministry, even if it is continuous. Regular meetings should supply the essential of regular TEACHING of the Word of God. It is not sufficient simply to **tear down** and overthrow strongholds of satan (2 Cor. 10:4) but it is essential to **build up** the Kingdom of God and the New Man within the human soul, otherwise God's work of RESTORA-TION is only half complete. It should be all part of the same Restoration package, with continuous PRAISE, THANKSGIVING, WORSHIP and FELLOWSHIP together with DELIVERANCE and BIBLE TEACHING.

It is all about LIVING in the Kingdom, WALKING in the Spirit, and being TRANSFORMED into the likeness of Jesus—NOW!

This will really challenge our Christian commitment because no genuine Christian who truly loves the Lord wants to be charged with playing games and hypocrisy. It is certain that every Christian who calls Jesus "Lord" is going to be shaken, tried and refined like gold (Job 23:10), and it is equally certain that those who continue to play religious games simply will NOT be part of the Bridegroom's marriage feast (Matt. 25:1-13).

We now come to a very important and often misunderstood subject—the estimating of the passage of TIME as it relates to Bible incidents of healings and miracles, and especially as recorded in the New Testament. I hope you will come to agree with me that this revelation alone is invaluable to your understanding of the Word of God.

CHAPTER 5

"TIME" IN THE NEW TESTAMENT

The notion that the New Testament presents us with a series of **immediate** healings and deliverances, at the very least, is highly questionable. Both healings and deliverances were not ALWAYS speedily concluded by a single word of command, although we usually understand the narrative that way because of the brief record of the incidents. For example, it is widely believed that the sermons of the apostles are recorded in only **brief** form as the Holy Spirit brought to **Luke's** mind the essentials of their messages. One can read **Peter's** sermon on the **Day of Pentecost** in approximately **three and a half minutes** and we are told that it resulted in three thousand conversions. I do not think that any Bible student seriously takes the view that Peter preached such a short sermon. In various places the passage of time creates some difficulties, e.g. Jesus' "short" prayer in the **Garden of Gethsemane**. It takes ten seconds to read the prayer as it is recorded in the New Testament but it is implied that Jesus prayed for three (3) hours (Mark 14:35-41, Matt. 26:39-45), that is, three sessions of one hour each.

How is this possible? The obvious answer is that the four points of Jesus' "short" prayer as recorded for us are simply the **main points** of Jesus' three hours of prayer as the disciples remembered them later. **The Bible can be spectacularly brief about dramatic incidents.**

Another example of this in **Gethsemane** is recorded as under:–

"Are you still sleeping? Take your rest. It is enough; the hour has come; the Son of Man is betrayed into the hands of sinners. Rise, let us be going..." (Mark 14:41-42).

Unless we understand that periods of time punctuate the text, we could be thrown into confusion. Jesus tells His disciples to take their rest and then He appears to say with His very next breath "That's enough!" But obviously there must be a space of time after the word 'rest'— perhaps 10 or 15 minutes or even more before He says to them "Enough... rise." And all this is recorded in half a dozen words.

Again it is a case of the bare details and principles of the actual incident being recorded for our benefit and it is very difficult to gauge the actual time elapsing without textual evidence. Similarly, it is very difficult to gauge the time that healings and deliverances took to accomplish, as the New Testament record of each incident is so brief and to the point.

The bare facts are given in almost logbook style. Consider for a moment the very heart of the New Testament, the Crucifixion of the Lord. How do the New Testament writers treat the actual crucifixion itself? If you or I had been eye-witnesses to the event, we would probably have written a book, or at least a chapter, on the details of the nailing to, and the erection of, the Cross, but as **Arthur Katz** points out, the Holy Spirit records it all in stark brevity—**"and they crucified Him"**.

Perhaps ten or even twenty dramatic minutes, recorded in FOUR words. We err greatly if we assume that all the incidents in the gospel narratives were instantaneous happenings, unless they are specifically recorded as such.

There are only five examples of **specific deliverance incidents** in the New Testament, so we do not have a wide range of choice when looking for examples of continuous, rather than instantaneous, success. However, what we have can be considered as vitally important KEYS to unlock our understanding of the ministry and they are very helpful, viz.:—

(i) THE MAN WITH THE LEGION

a) This incident, when all three gospels are harmonised, indicates a persistent attempt by Legion to avoid serious disadvantages, i.e.

(i) not to be tormented (Mark 5:7; Luke 8:28)

(ii) not to be sent out of the country (Mark 5:10)

(iii) not to be sent into the abyss (Luke 8:31) but finally—

(iv) to be sent into the swine (Mark 5:12; Luke 8:32)

All this took place (together with the question of name) **AFTER** the command to come out of the man (Luke 8:28-32; Mark 5:6-13). Let me repeat that—it is so important to our understanding. ALL THIS TOOK PLACE **AFTER** the command to come out!—indicating **protracted** opposition to the command of the Lord. How long did all the arguing take? The answer is, we don't know, but the point is that **overcoming opposition takes TIME.** Such was their rebellious state that even though they knew that they must bow the knee to the Holy One of Israel and depart in due course, they hung on to their dwelling place whilst "negotiating" their immediate future.

b) Matthew (8:31) uses a verb in the imperfect tense which gives the meaning "the demons besought Him continuously", **"kept begging Him"**, as **Father Lazarus Moore** translates the phrase for the **Russian Orthodox Church (Abroad).** The same repetition is indicated in Mark's account (5:10) where Mark not only uses the imperfect tense conveying "continuously" but also adds "much", which gives the sense of **continued and repeated** appeals by Legion (See **(ii)** on the translation of "polla").

It is reasonable to assume that any spirit which argues with the Lord Jesus Christ before obeying His direct command is going to give any disciple (learner) a hard time. The "single command" theory cannot be sustained from the account of the deliverance of the man with the Legion, and indeed **all the evidence points to a full-scale deliverance session.**

c) It is also interesting to note that **Kenneth Hagin** in his book **"I Believe in Visions"** records his encounter with Jesus in which the Lord explains some of the difficulties of His clash with Legion. While I do not take my stand on Kenneth Hagin's (or anybody else's) visions (Col. 2:18) it nevertheless confirms my own understanding of Legion's rebellion, viz:—

> *"Jesus said to Kenneth Hagin, 'to cast them out you sometimes have to know not only the kind of spirit but also their name and number. Notice that when dealing with the man from Gadara, I*

said 'come out of this man, thou unclean spirit',
but he didn't come out.' *This was something
I had completely overlooked in this Scripture
before, but on rereading the fifth chapter of Mark
I noticed that this was true. 'And he (Jesus)
asked him, what is thy name? And he answered,
saying, my name is Legion: for we are many'"
(Mark 5:9). ("I Believe in Visions" p. 79).*

(ii) THE EPILEPTIC, DEAF AND DUMB BOY

(Mark 9:14-29; Matt. 17:14-21; Luke 9:37-43)

a) One other detailed incident of Jesus performing
deliverance is the deaf and dumb epileptic boy. In his
record Mark uses the term **"polla"** which simply and
usually means **"much, many** or **great"**. The question is
"what does 'much' mean here?" Because most translators have never observed the deliverance ministry of
Christ in action, they have quite understandably chosen
"terribly" or "severely" as the appropriate translation.
However, **Father Lazarus** is a rather unusual man of
God in that he is both a translator AND experienced in
deliverance ministry. Therefore he chose to translate
"polla" with "repeatedly". This is not to say that the deliverance was not terrible or severe but simply adds another dimension to those two words—that of "many" or
CONTINUITY—so now we have the full picture of the
boy being **"convulsed repeatedly".** This gives us the
clue to a rather more prolonged deliverance than appears at first sight because the repeated convulsions
took place AFTER Jesus commanded the spirit to leave
(v. 25). Perhaps if the spirit had left in a single explosive
moment, the cure may well have been more damaging
than the infirmity, but this was not so.

As we said in chapter four there are many people receiving ministry who could not cope with a speedy deliverance. They have jobs to keep and a home to run, and to have a significant part of their personality torn down (even though it is anti-christ) can be quite a shattering experience if it happens all at once. **Progressive deliverance gives time** for the new creature to emerge and adjust to the increase of the Holy Spirit within. New **life-styles** have to be learned according to the New Covenant of the Lord Jesus Christ, and a **new discipline (discipleship)** of attending to Bible study, prayers and Christian fellowship has to be inculcated in people to whom all the kinds of things that Christians take for granted are brand new and even revolutionary. In other words, Jesus' ministry was to the congregation of Israel—steeped in God's word and already under tight religious discipline, but **today we often minister to people to whom submission, obedience and discipline are almost unknown,** and they have an enormous task before them—learning to put away their old rebellious life-style altogether and to put to death, to crucify the flesh, the old man and his ways. **This takes time and patience,** hence gradual deliverance gives an opportunity to taste of praise, worship, fellowship and teaching in gentle stages so that eventually the child of God has negotiated a miraculous transition from one who **receives** ministry to one who **gives out** to others. Some are quick, some are slow—God knows best.

In the matter of the deaf and dumb epileptic boy, no one can say (from the narrative) the length of the time indicated by the "convulsing repeatedly" in Mark 9:26, although Matthew's account indicates that it would have been no more than an hour. Unfortunately the phrase "in that hour" is sometimes translated "instantly" which I suggest, gives a false impression to readers of the English text of the Bible (Matt 17:18; see also 15:28). This is discussed further under the next heading.

b) It should also be borne in mind **the disciples failed in ministering to this case** and Jesus Himself said that *"this kind cannot be driven out by anything but prayer and fasting."* **It is apparent that prayer and fasting can only be effected over a protracted period of time.** Clearly there are some spirits that are so tenacious in maintaining the gates of the fortress of hades that Christians will find it necessary to **prepare themselves for a campaign** by prayer and fasting if they are to prevail, and this may include the subject receiving ministry.

(iii) THE SPIRIT OF A PYTHON

The only apostolic deliverance given in some small detail is the case of the woman with the **spirit of a python** (usually translated divination) which came out **in the same hour** (Acts 16:18). This, I suggest, is hardly the same as "immediately". It is a phrase used to indicate an approximate measure of time in the New Testament where time in society is measured by cocks crowing or positions of the sun rather than modern clockwork precision. It is worth noting that there is a Greek word for "immediately" (sometimes translated "straightway") the absence of which is significant, when we consider that Luke uses it on seventeen other occasions, BUT NOT HERE!

I understand that "in that hour" in Greek common usage of the day probably had a common meaning of "immediately", but we need to remember that the Holy Spirit inspired these words and **He doesn't deal in half-truths**

that need interpreting through temporal social customs. The evidence of "in that hour" is interesting and I believe supportive of my case, but the case we are building does not hang on this one point of interpretation.

Before concluding this section of our New Testament studies let me say that this whole book is saturated with New Testament evidence and I would be most uneasy and unhappy if it were not so, because the New Testament not only records for us the ministry of Christ and His apostles nineteen centuries ago but also prepares us for the present and future drama of End-Time salvation.

CHAPTER 6

END-TIME DELIVERANCE AND CLEANSING TODAY

At this point I hope you are able to agree that there is more in the New Testament narrative than first meets the eye. I trust that we have established **the enormous nature of a problem that has been hidden through the centuries, that of human demonisation,** and we are now moving towards a place where we can appreciate that incidents of healing and deliverance in the New Testament were not always the INSTANTANEOUS miracles we may have previously believed.

The time has now come to examine the second question put forward early in chapter 3. Now that we have a better understanding of the ministries of the Lord Jesus and the apostles nineteen centuries ago, we are in a better position to make an accurate comparison between the ministry of Christ THEN and Christ's ministry TODAY, which we understand to be an End-Time situation.

Obviously, where Christ's ministry of nineteen centuries ago is identical or similar to today's ministry there is no need for comment because Bible-loving Christians SHOULD ALL be in agreement in principle, if not in method.

It is important to be agreed in principles—methods are usually a matter of the traditions of men (e.g. the variety of baptismal formulae, but mostly incorporating the same basic principles). Therefore, in the matter of deliverance we should look into the New Testament for the principles but **shape the methods so that we can cope** with the mental and emotional needs of many times the number of people that were ministered to in New Testament days.

However, where there appears to be a difference IN PRINCIPLE, we must look at the Bible, at the matter of its historical content and God's Timetable. May I remind you of our comments in the section **"God's Unfolding Plan"**, and what was said there in relation to the progressive revelation of God through the Old and New Testaments also applies right up to the end of this dispensation and beyond, to the establishment of the New Heaven and the New Earth (Rev. 21:1).

So what do we say then, to the now often repeated question of "WHY CONTINUOUS ministry?"

Well, if we have caught the VISION spoken of in Chapter One we will have much of the answer. If we have understood and accepted the revelation of the PROBLEM in Chapter Three we will have even more of the answer, and if we have a new and more accurate understanding of the New Testament incidents a great deal of difficulty will be lifted away. But now we come to the place where certain differences between Christ's ministry nineteen centuries ago and today must be faced up to and examined. We can then go on to discuss some distinctive aspects of End-Time ministry as foreshadowed in the New Testament.

(i) HELPFUL COMPARISONS WITH NEW TESTAMENT TIMES

(a) Jesus' Primary and Secondary Missions during His earthly walk. His primary mission was obviously to

become the Sacrificial Lamb of God who took away the sin of the world by the giving up of His life on the Cross of Calvary. **Preaching the Kingdom of God** and **revealing God the Father** in His own person are other vital accomplishments. The working of healing, deliverance and other miracles are secondary to the main mission(s). They demonstrate the divinity of Jesus as the Son of God, the compassion of God and the reality of His Kingdom, and were not intended to do much more than that. They are secondary to the main reasons for his visitation in the flesh.

Therefore the Lord Jesus' prime mission was to defeat the powers of darkness, that is the **rulers, authorities** and **beggarly elemental spirits of the universe,** disarming them and making them a public spectacle by His Crucifixion (Col. 2:8-20). If they had known of this master Plan of the Ages they would never have crucified the Lord of Glory, but they did not know, and unwittingly carried out their part in God's plan of Salvation for us (1 Cor. 2:8).

Following on this we can say that **Jesus' ministry of salvation during His earthly walk was but a sample of what was and is to come,** as we today appropriate the victory of the Cross. Those demonstrations of the Kingdom of God were to the **obvious, external needs** of the people as they cried out for help. Today, with the revelation of God's Word in the whole of the New Testament we know that **human spiritual need[1] goes far deeper than healing the flesh or even removing destructive spirits of insanity** such as Legion, as our discussion of SIN revealed in Chapter 3.

---

[1] More fully discussed in Christian Deliverance Book 4 "Discerning Human Nature".

It is still the Lord Jesus' ministry today. It is not a case of what **He** did nineteen centuries ago compared to what **we** are doing now. It is a case of what **He** did then compared with what **He** is doing now and this, of course, is completely compatible with the **former and latter rain outpourings of the Holy Spirit,** spoken of by the prophet Joel (Joel 2:23). The latter rain blessing is far greater than the former, or if you like, **the blessings at the end of the Age will be far greater than the outpourings of the Holy Spirit at Pentecost** and through the Apostolic Age. These blessings, of course, will include a torrent of spiritual power through evangelism, healing and deliverance as the wedding preparations for the Bride of Christ are brought to completion and the Wedding Day approaches, so we can see that ministry today[1] will be a great deal more far-reaching than New Testament times.

No wonder Jesus said, *"Greater works than these will he (who believes) do, because I go to the Father"* (John 14:12).

Firstly, let us remind ourselves again that **we can do nothing good without the Lord** (John 15:5), and so, even though He talks about **us** doing greater works now than He did then, both He then and we now can only operate by the Power of the Holy Spirit working through us, and that Spirit is the Spirit of God and of Christ Himself. Therefore **it is not our doing the "greater works" at all, but He in us.** So many Christians are still reluctant to think they might be able to do works of greater miraculous impact than the Lord did while on

---

[1] Even as I revise this book in 1995, the Holy Spirit is being poured out across the world in what is called the "Toronto blessing".

earth and yet it is the same Spirit that raised Christ from the dead which dwells in us to do His will, so all things are possible to those who believe. Secondly, and most importantly for our discussion on deliverance, one of these greater works, I believe, is the **DEEP, INWARD CLEANSING OF THE BRIDE OF CHRIST** as she makes herself ready, and that, I assume, includes **You.**

The very fact that Jesus said His disciples would, after His departure, do greater works than He was doing must surely point to a **NEW DIMENSION OF MINISTRY.** If words have any meaning at all, these words of Jesus tell us that future ministries would not be limited to, but GO BEYOND what is recorded in the New Testament because, apart from conversions, the apostles did nothing more than Jesus accomplished in the flesh.

Now, if

(i) Jesus' words are true, and
(ii) We are living in the End-Time of this present Age,

and I do not doubt the truth of either of these statements, then **where is this new dimension of ministry?** As we look around the Church of God we may have noticed one thing at least, and that is the Lord's prophets have been saying for some time that **"the Lord is doing a New Thing"** (cf. Isaiah 42:9, 43:19, 48:6). In fact this has been so common-place in the last few years that one brother remarked after a meeting that "If I hear another prophecy about the Lord doing a New Thing I'll throw up (vomit)!" My response is that vomiting is as good a way as any for getting rid of a demon of unbelief. It is beginning to happen, NOW!

One problem is that many Christians do not really listen to prophecies when they come forth in an assembly, and even when they do they forget the Lord's Word when they go home (cf. James 1:23-24). The Lord has been saying He is doing a New Thing repeatedly, for years, but His people are so dull of hearing that many still do not really believe it, and have not received it. Prophecies should be tape-recorded, weighed (judged or discerned) and then typed and photocopied for interested Christians. Unfortunately so many Words from the Lord are lost on the same day they are given, but He is so gracious and patient to keep repeating this vital word UNTIL it cuts through our inner pollution like a sword and we become alive to it.

We should NOT BE SURPRISED at what is happening today.

This NEW THING relates to the Lord's mighty plan of SALVATION, DELIVERANCE and RESTORATION. Exciting isn't it, that we should be alive at this dramatic time in history—the time of the Bride making herself ready, and the time of the **"salvation ready to be revealed in the Last Time"** (1 Peter 1:5).

Time has run out for playing religious games. It's NOW or NEVER!

(b) Christ's Anointing and Ours

Another point to be considered, which may seem paradoxical to the first point, is that, compared with the Lord Jesus' ministry in the flesh, we have, at the moment, the ministry of babes. Yes, there are wonderfully anointed ministries across the world, perhaps not as many as we would wish, but the numbers of effective ministries seem to be growing, as is also the ANOINTING (provision of Holy Spirit power) on these ministries. However, the truth is that most ministries are still in the baby stage of their development compared with Christ's, as even the New Testament testifies that He was indeed **"anointed with power from above (more than) his partners"** (Heb. 1:9).

Take our own ministry, for example. In the early days, manifestations of unclean spirits leaving were looked upon as a great encouragement. We praised the Lord enthusiastically for the "wail of defeat" that came forth out of the sufferer, for we knew when that despairing wail signalled the departure of an unclean spirit. The manifestations were valued because we could see how the battle was going and knew when each victory was obtained. Later on, as the strength of the ministry increased, manifestations became embarrassing—all the flailing arms and feet, coughing and retching and all kinds of weird noises, some of them very loud—created a need for privacy and sound-proofing during ministry sessions. However, as the anointing increased even further we found that the Power of God blanketed the whole meeting and deliverance was obtained in the context of worship and praise of God, instead of only wails and screams. There is now hardly a flailing arm or a raised voice and if you were uninformed on the matter you would **sometimes** think that you had attended a praise meeting instead of a dynamic deliverance session. I don't say it will **always** be that way, but that is the way it is now, under the ministry's present level of anointing from above. However, even this seems to be changing again because my wife **Verlie** now carries the main anointing for deliverance and healing, under my headship, and she doesn't care so much if they are noisy, whereas I used to clamp down on them and demand that they leave quickly and QUIETLY!

It seems paradoxical to say on the one hand that today we shall do greater works than Jesus and yet on the other hand we today do not have the fullness of power to minister as effectively as He did, and yet it must be obvious that both these observations are true. The answer must be in what God called upon Jesus to do, to accomplish upon earth, and what He has called upon you and me to do. Jesus' own words give us the clue. We shall do greater works BECAUSE HE GOES (went) to THE FATHER. The three short years of Christ's ministry accomplished certain vital goals and **it is for His disciples to build upon the spiritual foundations He laid** and by **sheer measurement or opportunity of time,** if for no other reason, do the greater works He has planned, i.e. QUANTITATIVELY as well as QUALITATIVELY!

However, it is as well to be reminded that we are disciples of the great Teacher, i.e. we are learners. Let us visualise ourselves as having a great big "L for learner" plate hanging around our necks for all to see (and beware of!). I believe the Lord could have ministered deliverance more widely and more deeply than He did nineteen centuries ago, but it was NOT the **"Big Clean-Up" time—It was the "Pay the Price and Lay the Foundations" time,** which leads us on to our next point.

(c) Jerusalem or Babylon?

Yet another distinction between the ministry of Jesus on earth and His ministry today, is the KIND of people, with particular relation to their background, to whom He ministered. In New Testament times Jesus ministered to, with a handful of exceptions, **the people of Israel,** an Israel under the thumb of the ruling Pharisee party who were the conservative evangelicals of their day, exercising a rigid legalism over the lives of the Jews. For all their faults the Pharisees kept Israel a law-abiding, purist community so that a great deal of occult, idolatrous demonisation of the people, which could have been caught from the surrounding **Canaanites** and **Romans,** was avoided. Of course, they were demonised to some degree, as the gospels plainly testify, but nothing like as badly as the occult, idolatrous, Babylonian-style nations which surrounded them. We must now ask ourselves whether WE have descended from the comparatively spiritually "clean" and law-abiding Israelites to whom Jesus ministered, or from the corrupt, witchcraft-infested gentile nations of the inhabited world with their gods of sex, money, materialism, power, gambling, drugs and violence etc.

The conclusion I would feel obliged to draw is that **the ministry of deliverance today must, of necessity, be far more powerful and soul-searching than in New Testament times,** because our problems flow from our Babylonian-style cultures, rather than the monotheistic and God-fearing Jerusalem of old. Amen?

By now I trust you can accept that there are quite a number of points of difference between first century and twentieth century ministry, yet the Lord's work today is just as firmly based on the New Covenant as it ever was, for example:-

(ii)   GIFTS OF HEALINGS

Healings are listed as valid gifts of the Holy Spirit of

Christ for His body the Church in 1 Corinthians Chapter 12, and it is interesting to note that Paul (no doubt conscious of the many and varied ministries operating at the time, perhaps with vastly different methodologies and emphases, yet with the essential principles of faith in Christ being honored by the operation of the power of the Spirit) is careful not to call it a gift of healing but **uses a double plural, "gifts of healings"** (v. 9). So too today we observe a variety of gifts of healings emerging in the church from one side of the world to the other. That this plurality includes the deliverance ministry with its own variety of styles, yet with fundamental and biblical common ground, is also obvious when we observe that gifts of **"word of knowledge"**, **"miracles" (powers)** and **"discerning of spirits"** are also included in Paul's list of spiritual gifts in the same passage.

This variety of gifts is also demonstrated by the close affinity between **preaching, healing** and **deliverance** (casting out demons) in the ministry of Jesus, His commission to the disciples and their works as apostles. The Holy Spirit, perhaps by knowledge or discernment, will convict us at the appropriate time as to how to minister, and as sons of God we should be open to His leading on each occasion (Rom. 8:14), but as a general rule of thumb for "doubtful cases" (whilst experience in discernment is being obtained) prayer for physical healing could be offered in the first instance. If that ministry appears to be unsuccessful it is reasonable to assume that the spiritual resistance is caused by rulers and authorities and that specific deliverance may be necessary before healing can take place (cf. spirit of infirmity—Luke 13:10-17).

(iii) DISCERNMENT

When studying the deliverance in the case of the **python**

(divination) spirit it is worth noting that this woman followed Paul and Silas for MANY DAYS before Paul became sufficiently aware of her menace and DISCERNED the enemy within her (Acts 16:16-18). I think it is true to say that one of THE GREATEST SINGLE CAUSES OF DELAY OR LACK OF SUCCESS IN THE DELIVERANCE MINISTRY IS INADEQUATE DISCERNMENT. When considering the length of time the ministry sometimes takes, the efficient use of discernment (or lack of it) has to be taken into account, but bear in mind that VERY OFTEN THE LORD TAKES US THE LONG WAY AROUND to obtain the victory. For example, it took the Hebrews **40 years** to move out of Egypt and into the Promised Land of Canaan, when geographically it should only have taken a couple of weeks. "But" you say, "that was a unique or special situation. They needed to learn so much about faith and trusting God, about the Law of God and obedience to it." Yes, that is true for them **and it is also true for us.** Special situations or not, the point I am making is that with spiritual things, quick "solutions" promise much but can give you NOTHING. However, when the Lord takes us the LONG way around, THOSE WHO ARE FAITHFUL GET THERE AND RECEIVE EVERYTHING PROMISED! We too, have to learn about faith and trusting God. We too, have to receive the Law of Christ as revealed in the New Testament and live by it, or we too may die in a spiritual wilderness and never enter the blessing that God has prepared for us.

So not only does inadequate discernment cause delays and even failure, but sometimes the Lord's battle tactics can seem to cause delays. To illustrate again, it took seven (7) days for Jericho's wall to fall flat and the Hebrews to take the city (Joshua 6:12f). Someone might say that if the Hebrews had stormed the city on the first day it would have fallen within 24 hours—three days at the latest and they could have saved themselves four days or more on their invasion time-table. We who are Christians would say that God knows best and His way is the best way. Not only does it appear that the Hebrews did not suffer casualties but God's "slower" way obtained the victory whereas man's "quicker" way would have resulted, at best, in heavy casualties, or at worst, a siege lasting months, probably even ending in defeat. In other words, what seems to be a quicker way leads to nowhere but **God's way (fast or slow) is really quickest and best.**

Applying this principle to the deliverance ministry means that when God gives discernment on a certain problem, THAT is the way to minister. You may know what the **obvious** problem is, for example **epilepsy,** but the Lord may give you discernment of **spiritism.** If you minister His way you'll get rid of the spiritism, the epilepsy and whatever else lies in between. If you just tackle what is obvious—your way—you may find yourself on a spiritual treadmill with no end of the problem in sight.

The case of one subject who came to us is typical. She suffered from a massive infection of religious spirits which chattered incessantly in her head night and day and nearly drove her insane. After these were cleaned out other spirits were discerned, ministered against and eliminated. She improved and was able to work again while receiving ministry for the **eighth type of spirit** the Lord had searched out. Once deliverance has been claimed by a child of God, the Spirit of God apparently does not NOW, TODAY, want to cease His work until His temple is completely free and **this is a significant change**

from the old ways of ministry. It seems to be a NEW THING of mind-boggling significance, because it can only mean ONE THING—that **God has begun the preparation and the cleansing of the Bride of Christ for the Wedding Feast.** This continuous cleansing would now be the invariable experience of all those with whom we are associated in this ministry. Of course, a person may ignore the signals of the Holy Spirit and take whatever deliverance they came to get and go away without continuing in further ministry. Subsequent manifestations of unclean spirits should then taper off without causing too much undue discomfort, but of course that is to settle for "second-best". In fact this very matter raises an important question in deliverance work today and that is whether a Christian should ask the Lord for **SPECIFIC cleansing** or **TOTAL cleansing,** but either way it may take TIME. When we have ALL FAITH so as to move mountains and ALL DISCERNMENT, then we can expect speedy deliverance fairly regularly, but whether "speedy" ever becomes "instantaneous" in the matter of TOTAL cleansing remains to be revealed. No one has been perfected yet, to my knowledge, except legally!

(iv) SPECIFIC (PARTICULAR) DELIVERANCE

There is no doubt in my mind that the Bible gives us every encouragement to enter into **specific (particular) deliverance** for the cleansing out of unclean practices and habits, viz:–

"And a great house has not only vessels of gold and silver but also wooden and earthen, some for honour and some for dishonour.

IF THEREFORE ANYONE CLEANSES HIMSELF

> *from these (iniquitous practices and habits) he will be a vessel for honour having been sanctified, SUITABLE FOR THE MASTER, HAVING BEEN PREPARED for every good work.*
>
> *But flee from youthful lusts and pursue righteousness, faith, love, peace, WITH THOSE WHO CALL ON THE NAME OF THE LORD FROM A CLEAN HEART." (2 Tim. 2:20-22 lit.)*

Specific deliverance was evident in the ministries of the Lord Jesus and His disciples/apostles and is also available today, but as we have said, the Lord does not seem to want to minister in a patchwork kind of way any more and is encouraging His church to go for TOTAL CLEAN, but the "choice" rests with the individual Christian heart. **Specific** deliverance is still best achieved through continuous ministry, which ensures that nothing escapes attention, but everything commanded out is actually removed.

This type of deliverance is more for an "immediate needs" situation, as in the New Testament gospels. It just so happens that we are living in a time of history when our immediate needs are greater than we think, but because we do not know what tomorrow will bring forth we cannot see our immediate needs very clearly. Only God knows when the **Great Tribulation** will begin in earnest. Only God knows when the Church will be Raptured—and other events flowing around that great occasion. He knows our immediate needs better than we do, for He knows how imminent these and other dramas of the End-Time are! As we have already said, the fact of the matter is that time for this present dispensation has just about run out.

Therefore we can go to deliverance ministry and receive from the Lord the release for which we ask and go on our way rejoicing—if that is what we want. But if we have the Mind of Christ, and can capture the Vision of what is happening in our world within the context of the moving of God's Spirit across the earth, as everything accelerates, then we will want more than patchwork deliverance, we will want—

(v) TOTAL DELIVERANCE AND RESTORATION

What more is there to be said? You have either captured the Vision of the End-Time cleansing of the Church, the Bride of Christ, or you haven't. You have read the scripture about the church being presented without spot, wrinkle or blemish (Eph. 5:27) and, although you may have been taught that the Atonement of Christ achieves this perfection for the church, somehow a cleansing by covering over (atonement for) our sins may not sit too well on our Christian conscience as a COMPLETE explanation for this verse because the context implies TOTAL CLEAN inside and outside—without spot or wrinkle covered over. Not only that, but the apostle **Peter** makes it very clear to ALL Christians that this stage of perfection is **not simply a legal, positional truth, but a practical, experiential perfection** to be entered into by all who are looking for the coming of the Day of God and the new heavens and the new earth. He says

> ..."*therefore, beloved, since you look for these things, be diligent to be found by Him in peace, spotless and blameless*" *(2 Peter 3:11-14).*

This is not talking about our legal perfection in Christ

through justification by faith, but is an exhortation to make ourselves ready. **The imputed righteousness of Christ covering our sins is great news for all who have fallen asleep between the Cross and the Rapture, but we are now talking about those who will be caught up ALIVE to be with Christ without ever having tasted death (1 Thess. 4:17).** That is so important I implore you to read it again! After all, the Bride, who is also the King's daughter, will be **"all glorious WITHIN"** (Ps. 45:12 lit.) as well as having the imputed clothing of Christ's righteousness covering her on the outside.

Let me explain. The glorious Church Bride is to have **the clothing of the righteousness of Christ on the outside** and also **the cleansing of the Spirit of Christ on the inside.** This additional inner cleansing may seem like an "optional extra" which impinges upon the doctrine of justification by faith and other doctrines of Grace which flow from Christ's work on Calvary, but that is to misunderstand God's Master Plan of the Ages. It is just that our tiny minds tend to build brick walls around precious truths we have already received in the past, and we set limits to God in our understanding. We may be tempted to think that, because the Lord Jesus shed His Blood in order to atone for our sins and obtain for us our justification by faith, God's continued and expanded grace to us in removing, not just covering over, the sin within us is in some way an attack on the Atonement. However, nothing could be further from the truth. **The cleansing we Christians can now receive, the TOTAL INNER cleansing now available in THIS END-TIME, FLOWS FROM Christ's Victory on the Cross and in no way removes the need for His atoning Blood but, on the contrary, is built upon it.** Indeed if a sinner does not first personally appropriate the Sacrifice of

Jesus on Calvary, how can they enter into the blessing of inner cleansing and experience sanctification and RESTORATION? No, total deliverance is only possible for those who have been redeemed by the blood of the Lamb of God; that is, those who are justified by faith in the Blood of Christ.

Do not the scriptures themselves testify in many and various places and ways, that we are to be perfect as our Heavenly Father is perfect? Now God Himself is completing the gracious work He has begun in us as the Day of the Lord approaches.

(vi) THE KINGDOM OF GOD

One of the great, majestic themes of the Bible is **"the Kingdom of God"**. Writers of all shades of theological opinion have written never-ending pages on this glorious subject, but rarely to present it with its relationship to the ministry of deliverance. Yet it must be obvious that the growth of the Kingdom of God **on earth** is in direct relationship to the plundering of the kingdom of satan. Let us take a closer look at this relationship and the part that CONTINUOUS DELIVERANCE has to play in it.

(a) Definition

It is widely accepted in biblical circles that the phrase **"Kingdom of God"** is synonymous with **"Kingdom of Heaven"** (cf. Matt. 4:17 with Mark 1:15) as devout Jews, reluctant to use the term "God" for fear of blaspheming by using it flippantly, substituted the word "Heaven" in order to overcome their religious sensitivity. It is also understood that **"Kingdom"** means **"rule"**, so that "the Kingdom of God" does not refer simply to a geographical area but wherever God's rule, order or authority is set up over sin or pollution of any kind.

(b) The Kingdom of God and Deliverance

When Jesus is challenged by the Pharisees with using the power of Beelzebub, the Prince of demons, His reply includes the phrase **"If I by the Spirit of God cast out demons, then is the Kingdom of God come upon you"**. That is to say, the rule of God has displaced the rule of satan whenever demons are cast out (Matt. 12:26-28). What a glorious vindication of the deliverance ministry are these words of Jesus. In the face of all its detractors and critics, Jesus says to the Pharisees (today's and yesterday's) that if it is true we cast out demons by the SPIRIT OF GOD then in the very act of displacement of the unclean spirits by the Holy Spirit, the RULE OF GOD comes upon those involved. There are not too many ministries around of which that can be said with such confidence! Effective **evangelism, healing** and **deliverance—the three essential ministries of a full salvation**—would qualify, but we can confidently point to the Word of God and assert that **the Lord guarantees His Rule is always manifested in Holy Spirit deliverance ministry!**

This Kingdom or Rule of God in and over the human heart and mind obviously increases step by step as unclean spirits are cast out and the Holy Spirit is prayed in, and this infers a progressive growth. The question is, is this consistent with the Scriptures? The next section will show that it is.

(c) The Kingdom of God and Growth

The New Testament says of the Kingdom of God that *"it*

is like a grain of mustard seed which, when it is sown upon the earth, though it is less than all the seeds that are upon the earth, yet when it is sown, it GROWS UP and becomes greater than all the herbs, and it puts out great branches, so that the birds of heaven are able to dwell under its shade" (Mark 4:30-32; cf. Matt. 13:31-32).

It is plain that God's rule with the mustard seed has been one of growth—so slow that it is imperceptible to the human eye, but nevertheless so constant and real that what God created as very tiny, progresses into a mighty shrub. The mustard seed is used as a parable to describe faith (Matt. 17:20), the kind of faith that can move mountains. Faith can be very small, even tiny like a mustard seed, but when even tiny faith is placed in Jesus, it can achieve great things because the Rule of God is established where there is faith in Christ. The Rule or Kingdom of God is a **continuously growing Kingdom today.**

Therefore as faith brings deliverance and satan is banished, so the Rule of God comes more and more upon the object of His grace—sometimes quickly and suddenly—sometimes slowly as a matter of constant growth. Jesus describes this **gradual progression as "first the blade, then the ear, then the full grain in the ear"** (Mark 4:28).

Thus, continuous deliverance ministered today is completely in accord with the continually growing Kingdom of God, for wherever demons are cast out to the glory of the Lord Jesus, there and then has the Kingdom of God come upon us! Praise His Holy Name!

One further point is worth mentioning. What we have said about the Kingdom of God and its continuous growth should be the normal situation for every Christian who is abiding in the Word of God and living the life of a true disciple. We all know that one never stands still in life, whatever our field of endeavour. We either go forward or we go backwards and it is no different in our spiritual lives. We either go forward into the unsearchable riches of Christ or we drift into forgetfulness, becoming dull of hearing and blurred of sight as we allow the flesh to overtake the spirit.

If we are one of those who stay close to God, continuously learning new things from His Word and being led by His Spirit, there will be a continuous release taking place in our lives, freeing us from the things of the world more and more. This is normally thought of as "growing in grace" or "Christian maturity" and it is a most important aim for the sincere Christian. We ALL ought to aim for this continuous increase of the Kingdom of God in our lives because as it takes place the kingdom of satan is diminished in us.

Thus, EVERY CHRISTIAN WHO IS INCREASING IN THE TRUE KNOWLEDGE AND THINGS OF GOD IS EXPERIENCING SPIRITUAL RELEASE from satan and his powers of darkness and is therefore OBTAINING A MEASURE OF AN INVISIBLE DELIVERANCE, WHETHER OR NOT THE SPECIFIC MINISTRY OF DELIVERANCE IS INVOKED OR COMMANDED.

Many times I have sat in church assemblies where the praise of God has brought down the power of the Holy Spirit and hundreds of "invisible" deliverances have been taking place all around me. On one occasion a pastor

·was preaching an inspired sermon and the power of God fell, making everyone in the assembly feel drowsy. He stopped in the middle of his message and said, "My, what a sleepy lot you are today. Did you all have late nights"—not realising it had nothing to do with the flesh but was of the Spirit of God! They were all set up for a mighty outpouring of healing and deliverance, had the preacher been aware of what was happening and how to proceed. What a lot we have yet to learn. There is still a long way to go for each and every one of us who seeks to serve the Lord in this End-Time.

However, beware a temptation! Praise, worship, preaching and other ministries may change our lives dramatically over the span of a life-time and bring us to a MEASURE of deliverance by removing **worker-class** and, perhaps, even some **middle-class** spirits but they can never take the place of specific, anointed deliverance ministry. And today, of course, there is no more time to play games. It is time to be delivered of **rulers and authorities,** and quickly too. **There is no time left to take 40 years to become like Jesus!**

In conclusion, if we can accept that the increase of the Kingdom of God in our hearts and lives is an imperceptible, invisible, continuous increase, and also recognise that deliverance brings the Kingdom of God upon us, according to the Word of God, then it seems to me that the idea of receiving continuous deliverance should pose no problem to any thoughtful Christian, especially now that the deliverance ministry can be combined with normal worship, teaching and fellowship in the regular assembly.

When it all boils down, is it not a matter of TRUSTING the

Lord and OBEYING His Commands to be CLEANSED and PERFECT? (See Appendices, especially D and G).

(vii) THE "TORONTO" BLESSING

This present outpouring of the Holy Spirit is so called because the airport church at Toronto, Canada is reported to have had **90,000 visitors** through its doors within a period of 18 months, all seeking or inquiring about a fresh touch from the Holy Spirit. It is a media, not a Christian label.

Christians from all over the world have passed through its doors, received a fresh touch and taken the blessing to their home church. However, the questions remain— **what lasting value is it, and what are God's purposes for it at this time in history?**

(a) The Stages of Revival

I am suggesting there are at least four stages in a genuine Revival. They are:

(i) **The Preparation Stage,** when the prophets of God speak forth what God is planning to do (Amos 3:7), usually in broad terms, like the NEW THING prophecies. **Prophets from all over the world have been "warning" of the coming Revival for at least 20 years**, and more urgently in the last 2 years. If Christians have been caught by surprise it is because they do not listen to the prophets or have not believed them.

(ii) **The Honeymoon Stage** is on now, as I write. People can get an easy blessing with little or no price to pay. Many do not understand that **with blessing comes responsibility and a new commitment to service and discipleship**. What they do not understand at the beginning they will understand soon enough (cf. Mark 9:26-27)! Some will fall away.

Praise the Lord that many will catch fire and want to continue in Christ AFTER the honeymoon is "over". There will be TRUE repentance and the fruit that it brings forth (Luke 3:7-9).

(iii) **The Teaching (Theological battle) Stage** is just beginning. Some fine and respected international Bible Teachers will oppose the movement, mainly due to mis-interpreting the manifestations of laughter (some Holy, some unclean) roaring, shaking, passing out on the floor[1], running on the spot etc. (cf. Mark 9:26-27).

The simple fact is that **the Lord is sovereignly kick-starting (or jump-starting) His cleansing deliverance program in His people on a worldwide basis,** overruling His shepherds, many of whom have hung back from the real task of preparing the Bride.

Not only is there misinterpretation of the manifestations (symptoms) but there is also an inbuilt legalism in many denominational leaders that **always resists the Holy Spirit** (Acts 7:51) until it is overcome in the human will by the Spirit Himself, and broken.

---

[1] See Christian Authority and Power pages 18-28.
Christian Deliverance Book 1, chapter 1,1.
Christian Deliverance Book 2, chapter 5.8 for fuller discussion.

(iv) THE SERIOUS CLEANSING STAGE

Here is the Vision yet again.

... **the perfecting of the saints** (believers)
... **to the measure of the stature of the fullness of Christ** (Eph. 4:12-13)
... **through spiritual (inner) cleansing** (James 4:8, 2 Peter 3:13-14)
... **by Deliverance and Restoration programs** (Rom. 12:2, 2 Cor. 7:1)
... **in the Name of the Lord Jesus Christ** (Col. 3:17).

When we see programs implementing this vision throughout the Body of Christ, and especially the Renewal churches, THEN we should begin to look for the visible emergence of the five wise maidens.

After that, when we see the Body of Christ divided, split 50-50 over personal, inner cleansing, the wise and the foolish, THEN we can expect the Trumpet of God to blow soon (1 Thess. 4:15-17).

(b) Nine Important Principles

Do you remember the incident where Jesus delivered (Mark 9:25) and healed (Matt. 17:18, Luke 9:42) a young lad who was **dumb, deaf and epileptic?** (Matt. 17:14-20, Mark 9:14-29, Luke 9:37-43). We present you some of the key verses from Mark, chapter 9.

I brought to you my son who has a dumb spirit, and wherever it takes him it dashes him down, and he foams, and grinds his teeth and pines away (vs. 17-18).

*And they brought him to Jesus, and when he (the boy) saw him (Jesus) immediately **the spirit tore him severely, and he fell on the ground and wallowed, foaming.** (v.20).*

*... Jesus rebuked the unclean spirit, saying to him, "You dumb and deaf spirit, I command you come out of him and enter him no more!" **And having cried out and torn him repeatedly he came out, and the boy became as one dead**, so that the majority said "He is dead".*

But Jesus took him by the hand, and raised him up, and he arose. (vs. 25-27).

(Up-date of the Revised Version).

This incident is so rich in teaching material for us. When studying how the power of God works together with the deliverance ministry it is obvious the Lord Jesus ministered deliverance and healing to hundreds, even thousands, of sufferers, yet we only have four or five incidents recorded in any detail.

This makes each incident we have been given an essential KEY that opens many doors (revelations) for us, and merits the most careful attention!

Learning the lessons of **Mark 9:26-27** we can see that **going under or manifesting the Power of God:**

1. Does **NOT** mean you are a higher grade, super-spiritual Christian.
2. It means the OPPOSITE. **You NEED MINISTRY.**
3. Makes tough deliverances, which are **SPIRITUAL surgery**, easier and (sometimes) quieter.

4. Means the deeper the anaesthetic, the deeper the ministry needed. (cf. Gen. 2:21).
5. Is **NOT** a quick-fix, but it is a **beginning!**

ALSO

6. This ministry **must NOT be avoided.** We are to avoid formal religion and religionists. We are **NOT** to avoid ministries of God's power! (2 Tim. 3:2-5).
7. This ministry **must NOT be forbidden** (Mark 9:38-40).
8. Most observers will get it wrong at the beginning.
9. Most Pharisees will **ALWAYS** get it wrong! (Acts 7:51).

(c) Summary

Thanks be to God, He has broken into the traditions of the churches with a fresh wave of power, apparently flowing from the **Vineyard Church at Toronto airport.**

What we in little Full Salvation Fellowship, Sydney could never do (by ourselves) the good Lord has done sovereignly, pouring out His power and flattening people, with attendant healings and deliverances. This is not new, of course. **Renewal churches have known this power for about twenty-five years** but I have no hesitation in saying that they have not known what to do with it. It has been used as a gimmick to attract crowds into churches. It has been used to exalt the ministers with this "gift". **What it has NOT yet been used for is the reason for which it has been given, that is, to begin the serious cleansing of the saints,** ALL who wish to be included in the Bride of Christ.

Even with the sovereign deliverance and healing of some, the penny still hasn't dropped what God is wanting to do. However things are gathering speed. This move of the Spirit is spreading with amazing speed, from **Argentina to Siberia**, from the **U.S.A. to Australia**. Because of its misuse in the past some Christians have questioned its source (inspiration) and genuineness. That is perfectly understandable and indeed healthy. I suggest a study of the power of God as presented in our publications **"Christian Authority and Power"** (written about fifteen years ago!) or **Christian Deliverance Book 2 "Engaging the Enemy"**, which describes similar outpourings during the **Wesleyan Revival**, as a starting point.[1]

What has the Lord got to do to wake up His shepherds to the need for inner (soulish) cleansing for EVERY ONE OF GOD'S CHILDREN—INCLUDING THEMSELVES!?

We are talking serious, week by week refining in the fire of God's Deliverance and Restoration programs for everyone in every Renewal group and church making up the five wise maidens!

Through Pastors like **Rodney Howard-Browne, John Arnott, and many others** the Lord is giving His people a fresh beginning—let's not waste it again.

PRAYER FOR TODAY'S REVIVAL

Dear Lord, help me not to feel left out when you are blessing others, but to enter into their blessings and rejoice, in Jesus' Name, Amen.

---

[1] Even before reading these publications, we recommend "TORONTO and The Truths You Haven't Heard Before."

CHAPTER 7

CONCLUSIONS

What have we said in support of the people of God submitting themselves to CONTINUOUS cleansing deliverance ministry?

These are the facts as we see them:

1.   The Lord has inspired over the last few years a number of deliverance ministries around the world which are developing under His continuing and increasing anointing of POWER. Now He is breaking through EVERY OBSTACLE with the promised REVIVAL!

2.   These ministries, in particular those with whom we have personal experience, have discovered something of the enormous demonisation of mankind. The variety of unclean spirits, the widespread extent of their influence, and the numbers that can be involved in ONE human are almost unbelievable.

However, these discoveries are quite consistent with the teaching of the Word of God. To the accusation that we see demons under every stone, we may well plead "guity" but what we see in the spirit has not been of our own choosing. We see what God has enabled us to see and, although the spiritual problems of the world look horrific, nevertheless we are comforted in the sure knowledge that those who are for us are more than those who are against us (2 Kings 6:15-17) invisible though they may be to most.

The truth is that most of us have never really understood

or believed the apostle John when he wrote that **"the whole world lies in (the power of) the evil one"** (1 John 5:19) or the apostle Paul when he wrote that **"we are not contending with blood and flesh but with (spiritual) rulers and authorities..."** (Eph 6:12) and **"...anything that is not of faith is sin"** (Rom. 14:23) or even the Lord Jesus when He said not to make promises or oaths that you may not be able to keep. **Anything more than a "yes" or a "no" is evil** (Matt 5:33-37), because it is only by God's grace we can keep any commitment, and we have no guarantee of tomorrow.

You can quickly see that, as far as God's Word is concerned, evil has had a profound and enormous influence on all our lives—more than we were aware of or ever thought possible.

3.   Our vision and understanding of the Cross is enlarged, not diminished, by the ministry of deliverance. When we realise that Christ Jesus defeated our spiritual enemies on the Cross and put them to shame (Col. 2:15), then we begin to appreciate what the full victory of the Cross really means. It gives us an understanding of the overwhelming nature of the victory of the shed Blood of Calvary that rendered all this ugly power, all these principalities, the world rulers of this present darkness, as something to be trodden on under our feet (Luke 10:19). The more we look at the scripture and the deliverance ministry the more the wonder of the Cross is enlarged and magnified, and **to put down deliverance is to reduce the victory of the Cross.** To minimise deliverance presumes that the enemy is not so widespread, that he is only a little enemy with a tiny kingdom that might occasionally come to attack us, and in the West, of course, we don't have to worry about

that! It is only the primitive, poor, disease-ridden people of the world who need the missionaries and perhaps deliverance (they say). You know that is not true, and I know it's not true. To minimise demonology is to minimise the victory. If we say that demonisation is rare in the West except for some mental cases, and it is only the primitive people on the mission fields who need deliverance we:

(i) deceive ourselves, and therefore

(ii) unwittingly denigrate Christ's redeeming work on the Cross, and

(iii) are tragically inhibited in our diagnosis of the spiritual needs around us.

If we understand the true composition and meaning of the root disease of SIN (Gen. 4:7, Matt. 12:38-45), and if we take Paul's words (Eph. 6:12, 2 Cor. 10:3-4) as literal statements of truth, it becomes very difficult to sustain the view that cases of demonisation are rare, rather the evidence supports the view that FREEDOM from demonisation is rare.

It is this very concept which has created opposition towards our deliverance ministry, and there is understandably an enormous reluctance to face the mind-boggling consequences of this truth, as it reaches into every Christian family, but surely pastoral observation supports what we believe the Bible is saying. Suffering Christians can be counselled by faithful and patient ministers for 20 years or more, and although such pastoral support is often gratefully received and a source of strength over the long years of adversity, nevertheless all too often the end result is disappointing. **What is usually achieved is SURVIVAL; what is usually NOT achieved is a CHANGE of heart or a change from adversity and sickness to victory and health.** It has never been God's will for Christians to simply SURVIVE but to be OVERCOMERS and CONQUERORS in love, joy and peace.

Such counselling is usually applauded by the church for its "stickability", rather than criticised for ineffectiveness, and rightly so, for we each can only do our best according to the light we have from God. Likewise with **continuous healing.** The Church at large, with the exception of certain pockets of extreme pharisaism, has had no difficulty in supporting or practising continuous healing. Most of the great healing ministries of the world to date, such as that of the late **Kathryn Kuhlman,** abound in testimonies of progressive healing,[1] and the only Christians with raised eyebrows are those who have difficulty in believing in any form of supernatural intervention and personal blessing from their God. To them He is more a legal guardian God than Father God.

Yet when we come to the specific ministry of deliverance, which after all is included in the many "gifts of healings" (1 Cor. 12:9) being healing of the soulish (psychical) area (mind, emotions, memory etc.), so few Christians perceive the inconsistency between applauding **continuous healing** and criticising **continuous deliverance.**

People who criticise continuous deliverance ought to consider the results it obtains over both the short and long term with a large number of "difficult" cases (the

---

[1] "I Believe in Miracles" by Kathryn Kuhlman, pp. 34-35. 80-82.

sort of problems most churches put into their "too hard" file) and compare them with the results obtained by continuous counselling on similar case histories.

Pastors seem to have as much difficulty as other Christians in this matter, perhaps because to recognise the truth of what I have said should result in a significant shift of emphasis, not only in one's ministry to others but also in one's personal pursuit of holiness and crucifixion with Christ.

I remember an incident with one Pastor which left me speechless. When I asked him if he believed in continuous healing he said "Yes". Good, I thought, he'll have to agree to continuous deliverance, but when I posed the question, he stunned me by replying "No". The conversation ceased abruptly (but not disagreeably) at that point because he had nothing more to say (what COULD he say that made sense!) and such inconsistency left me dumbfounded. What may be even more illogical is that, in spite of the episode above I still admire and respect his shepherd's heart. The Lord hasn't finished with him yet, or me either for that matter.

However when it comes to **criticism,** those who criticise may not know what manner of spirit they are of (cf. Luke 9:51-55)[1] and need to remember that **the Kingdom of God consists not in talk (logos) but in POWER** (1 Cor. 4:20) and that power flows from the victory of the Cross of Christ Jesus! Thus **understanding deliverance enhances and honours the finished work of Christ.**

---

[1] If your Bible does not include these verses in full, check its marginal notes or footnotes, or change your translation.

4. The Lord's solution to such widespread demonisation is to now reveal not only the problem but also the solution, which is **His Great Salvation** (Heb. 2:3) **"ready to be revealed in the last time"** (1 Peter 1:5). This Great Salvation of spirit, soul and body is by the ministries of evangelism, deliverance and healing.

5. Therefore **the Spirit of God seeks to cleanse the children of God in their souls,** in their inward parts, and will minister deliverance continuously to those who **seek to purify themselves** into the likeness of the Son of God, so that when they see Him they will be like Him (1 John 3:2-3, 2 Tim. 2:21, James 4:8). Blessed are the PURE OF HEART, for they shall see God (Matt. 5:8).

6. Whether a Christian seeks **particular** cleansing, or **total** cleansing, it is evident from the testimony of both the Old Testament and the New Testament that many deliverances, whether from physical enemies in Joshua's day or spiritual enemies in Jesus' and the apostles' earthly walk, were little-by-little or speedily progressive rather than instant transformation, so there is ample biblical precedence for what is happening in our ministry and in other ministries also. **Frank and Ida Mae Hammond** record in their deliverance book **"Pigs in the Parlor"** their admiration of schizophrenics who fight through to victory over a period of time (pp. 124, 133) *"—sometimes several months or even a year, or longer"* (p. 129).

7. **THE RESPONSE of the sufferer** can be very important in relation to the progress that they are making, whether with deliverance or healing or both. I can think of ten (10) areas requiring a positive response of faith:

      (i) The **sincerity** of the sufferer in desiring the

ministry, regardless of all discouragement, doubt and fear ministered by well-meaning Pastors and Christians, or false brethren, who have not caught the vision, etc. (Eph. 6:10-14, Phil. 3:2, 3:17-4:1).

Also the sufferer's ability to:

(ii) **Catch the revelation of God** about sin and demons, and the extent of our infection, i.e. to understand something of the PROBLEM. Sin and rebellion are demonic (Gen. 4:7, Matt. 12:28-45, Eph. 2:2, 6:12).

(iii) **Know when they are manifesting** uncleanness (Matt. 15:18-20).

(iv) **Bring their spiritual Christian weapons into operation** when they are under spiritual attack (i.e. manifesting). For example, Praise, Prayer, Authority, Word, etc. (James 4:7-8, Matt. 18:18, 1 Cor. 12:4-11, Eph. 6:14-18, Phil. 4:4-9).

(v) **Cope with manifestations and actual deliverance day by day** in view of their ongoing responsibilities at work and at home. (Rom. 8:31-39, Phil. 1:27-30, 3:12-17, 4:13).

(vi) **Follow the counselling** given, putting away and **overruling all rebellious inclinations of self-will** (Phil. 2:12-13, Heb. 13:7,17).

(vii) **Trust those who are ministering** BEYOND the counselling given, even more than THEIR

118

OWN ideas, to the point of discarding deceptive notions when required, that is, the teaching of demons (Prov. 3:5, John 10:4,5,14, 2
Cor. 8:5, 1 Tim. 4:1).

(viii) **Keep looking ahead** to the ultimate victory,
and not looking back (with longing) until it is
achieved, i.e. the personal **determination TO
WIN** in the name of the Lord Jesus (Luke 9:62,
Gal. 6:9, Phil. 3:12-4:1, Rev. 2:1-3:22).

(ix) **REJOICE in the SOLUTION** provided by
Jesus Christ our Lord, to **see the vision of
the End-Time clearly for the whole true
Church**—and rejoice in belonging! (Matt. 25:1-
11, Phil. 4:4-7, 1 Thess. 5:16-18, James 1:2-
4, 1 Peter 1:5-9).

(x) **Keep the Word of God** in the New Covenant
and **walk in the spirit/Spirit,** more and more,
moment to moment (John 3:36, Gal. 5:16-25,
Eph. 5: 15-20, Phil. 1:27-2:2). **This is true
discipleship!**

I think it needs to be said that whether miracles happen
quickly or slowly, there is no way every observer is going
to be satisfied. The Lord Jesus exercised a dynamic
ministry in the power of the Spirit and yet He had legions
of critics (cf. John 15:23-25). It is hard for the tradi-
tionalist, indeed any of us, to kick against the goads
and **the Pharisee Saul** even had to be blinded for three
days to show him what real darkness was all about, and
to draw his attention to his true spiritual state before he
could become **the great apostle Paul.** You may not be
able to accept all the evidence presented here, but its

presentation will be considered worthwhile if you are brought to the point where you can say, "fast or slow, bless your people Lord—do it YOUR way. Increase your Rule in our lives—have thine own way!"

Deliverance and Sanctification (Holiness)

We have to ask ourselves what is the relationship, if any, between the deliverance ministry and the sanctification of a Christian.

The **I.V.F. Bible Dictionary** tells us that the word **'sanctify'** comes from the Latin 'to make holy' and the Hebrew 'to set apart' or 'brightness'. This latter meaning may seem strange to us but the Dictionary goes on to say that *"brightness may underlie those usages which relate to condition, state, or process, leading on in the New Testament to the thought of **an inward transformation gradually taking place, resulting in purity,** moral rectitude, and holy, spiritual thoughts expressing themselves in an outward life of goodness and godliness."*

While we might properly say that 'normal' sanctifying methods such as Bible study have in the past helped Christians to CONTROL the sin problem within them, the deliverance ministry of Christ REMOVES the problem altogether. It must therefore be obvious that deliverance should be a major weapon used for the sanctifying of the growing Christian today.

Somehow, we have to get across to the Body of Christ the message that deliverance ministry is not just a spectacular extra added onto an evangelistic meeting in order to impress the ignorant with the

reality of the risen Lord, although that is quite legitimate. It has an even more important function for the informed people of God in the ongoing life and development of the Church, especially now, in the End-Time.

Do I hear someone saying that you want a scripture reference before you accept this idea? Please refer to Matthew 15:21-28 where two central points emerge from the story of the deliverance of the **Canaanite woman's daughter:**

(i)   Deliverance is for **God's Covenantal people FIRST,** and then available for NON-COVENANTAL people IF they manifest faith in the Lordship of Jesus.

(ii) Jesus, who is the Living Bread, describes the deliverance ministry He is being asked to perform as BREAD—that is, **as essential to the people of God as their daily physical bread.**

At the moment we are seeing people change as much in four (4) years as they would normally change in forty (40) years, and we expect the Lord to reduce this four year intensive sanctification period even further as the End of the Age draws closer.

Does this sound great to you and are you praising the Lord? Good, but two words of caution:

(i)   Even after forty years of sanctification we will still seem to fall far short of the perfection of the Lord Jesus, and

(ii) Each Christian is, in the final analysis, responsible for their own rate of progress, according to their commitment, obedience (action) and submission (attitude).

Remember the definition of **'Sanctify'?** The Deliverance ministry is also for the achieving of **an inward transformation, gradually taking place, resulting in purity...** In other words its main use ought to be for the inner cleansing and transformation of EVERY CHRISTIAN, that is, FOR OUR SANCTIFICATION. (Eph. 5:25-27).

Someone may ask, "Will some Christians miss out on the Rapture because they have been newly converted and don't have time to get cleansing deliverance?" The answer is NO. In that day there will be many "people of power" in the Body of Christ whom God can use to minister a speedy work to new converts so that no one need be afraid of missing out on "total clean" because of late conversion or a late start. Our Father will provide for His faithful children. What we must avoid at all costs is being included in the five (5) foolish virgins who had the door of the Wedding Feast of the Bridegroom shut tight in their faces BECAUSE THEY HAD NO OIL IN THEIR LAMPS (Matt. 25:1-13). I take this to mean that due to playing the fool with the world they were not truly CLEANSED and FILLED with the Holy Spirit, or to put it another way, they had not made themselves ready. The most solemn warning to come from the Lord's teaching through this parable is that perhaps **even 50%—HALF of the Church which has tasted of the Holy Spirit at some time or another, not just nominal churchgoers—will have allowed their love for the Lord to grow cold.** The consequences for the five foolish virgins are terribly sad, so let us resolve NOT to be found amongst them, but rather amongst the wise virgins who were READY and WAITING for the Bridegroom.

I am going to say without any apology whatever, that **continuous ministry is necessary for God's people everywhere if the Bride of Christ is to be thoroughly**

cleansed, prepared and beautiful, ready for the Bridegroom. And not only ready for the Bridegroom but also ready for PERSECUTION and the Great Tribulation. For if they persecute Christians when things are tolerably good what will they do when things are bad and their lives are in the balance? (Luke 23:28-31).

The only way I can foresee continuous ministry being unnecessary in these last days is if, in the gracious provision of the Lord, He anoints and empowers various ministers of every nation, tribe and tongue, to minister total and speedy cleansing. Perhaps the present wave of Holy Spirit Revival will lead up to this? Many have thought they were doing this, but the truth is we have had no real concept of the magnitude of the task or the meaning of the WHOLE COSMOS lying in the power of the evil one (1 John 5:19) and therefore many have been deceived.

Do not be discouraged at this, for the greater the task, then (1) the greater the salvation provided by our Lord Jesus, (2) the greater the glory for the Godhead, and (3) the greater joy we can have as we are called to be the earthen vessels through which the Holy Spirit will achieve the Great Salvation of God, which the whole earth shall see.

Hallelujah!

Beloved, the Lord calls you and me to REPENT, to purify ourselves as He is pure so that when we see Him we shall be like Him.

........and the time is SHORT,

so

what are you doing about it!

For further reading, "TORONTO and the Truths You Haven't Heard Before" by this author, and "Those Who Love Him" by Basilea Schlink.

INVITATION

WHAT DO YOU DO NOW?

If you have caught something of the Vision that the Lord has shown to us, and the Holy Spirit has convinced you that YOU should be included amongst those whom the Lord will cleanse and prepare for His coming, then do not be afraid, double-minded, distracted or delayed by ANYTHING or ANYONE!

Do not think that you are unworthy or that your sins have been too great or that there are many better or holier people than yourself who should be ministered to before yourself—that is NOT the way the Lord looks at things at all. You may not even be a Christian or you may be uncertain about such things as where you stand with the Lord, but those things of the past don't matter right now. The Lord Jesus has told us plainly that many who are first shall be last and the last first, that many shall come from North, South, East and West to enter the Kingdom of God BEFORE some of the religious leaders of the day (Luke 13:28-30). He said that even such unlikely people as the despised **tax-gatherers** (for the conquering Romans) and **harlots** will enter the Kingdom of God BEFORE the Chief Priests and elders of the church of the day (Matt. 19:23-22:14) because they believed the Word of God preached by John the Baptist and repented (that is, changed the direction of their lives towards God). The religious leaders, bound by the leaven of the Pharisees, for all their knowledge of the scriptures, failed to do just that (repent and believe) but held to their dogma and justified themselves in their own eyes.

So, you see, your **previous** situation is not important in

124

the eyes of the Lord. What is important is that YOU believe that God is working out His plan to judge the earth and save for Himself as many as will repent and ask for mercy, and YOU REPENT and ASK FOR MERCY—the sooner the better. How about right now?

If you are not a Christian or if you are a Christian who has been slack and failed to follow the Lord Jesus the way you know you should, then you can put things straight with the Lord by saying a prayer along the following lines:

Dear Lord Jesus,

I am a sinner and I now know that I have done things which have grieved you. I am truly sorry Lord, for my sins.

Please forgive me for ALL my sins. Wash me clean in your precious Blood. I renounce the devil, the powers of darkness and all their works.

I ask you, Lord Jesus, to break every foul curse upon my life, snap every unclean chain that binds me. Please FILL ME with your HOLY Spirit of power, and set me free to worship you and serve you as I should.

Thank you, Lord Jesus, for making it all possible for me on Calvary's Cross, my Lord and my God.

Hallelujah and Amen!

Don't READ this prayer out to the Lord but examine it and pray its PRINCIPLES out loud, from your HEART, using your own words. Don't say it if you don't **mean** it.

This is a beginning, or a fresh start!

After this prayer has reconciled you to your Heavenly Father through the Lord Jesus Christ, **you must move into contact with ALIVE Christians as soon as possible,** preferably those who share the same kind of vision as in this book. There is not much point in joining a Church which belongs to the five foolish virgins group— they won't help you get clean and ready. If you have any difficulty or even if everything goes smoothly for you, please 'phone us or write to us and tell us what you have done.

We know that God will provide a way forward for you to enter into the move of God's Spirit today and possess all that you want to possess. The only limitations are what you yourself impose, perhaps by failing to link with others who have caught fire.

We are here to help you if you need us.

GOD BLESS YOU.

Peter and Verlie Hobson

P.O. Box 1020
Crows Nest 2065
N.S.W., Australia

Phone: (02) 9436 3657
Fax: (02) 9437 6700

APPENDIX A

AMERICAN PROPHECIES

PROPHECIES FROM THE MINISTRY OF J. LELAND EARLS, WASHINGTON, U.S.A.

Introduction (by J. Leland Earls):

... These prophecies relate to your own personal spiritual preparation for the trying days that are ahead. Only a fool would go into battle as a soldier with no preparation, or into an athletic contest with no training. Yet millions of Christians are going to get caught with little or no spiritual preparation for the tribulation days ahead when more will be required of God's people than at any other time in human history. **There is nothing more important for your life now than for you to let the Lord prepare you for the days that are shortly coming.**

Read Luke 12:31-48 (especially), but it would be well to read and meditate on the whole chapter. Notice verse 42, which speaks of that "faithful and wise steward" whose responsibility is to give out what is called the "meat in due season". In its **first** application that "steward" is the Holy Spirit who is being faithful to make known that specific "meat" or spiritual revelation for this end-time. Much concerning His plan and purpose, God has reserved for **this specific time** in human history, and the Holy Spirit as the "faithful steward" is now making known this "meat in due season". In its **second** application that "steward" is represented by **those special ministries which God has raised up in this hour with a special commission to receive this end-time revelation by the Spirit and make it known unto those who will hear.** That which you have received through these publications is a portion of that "meat" for this hour. In its **third** application that "steward" is **YOU. You have a responsibility to be faithful in that which you are receiving.** You have a special stewardship in this end-time, and **it is imperative that you not only prepare yourself but also help to prepare others.** You cannot escape this responsibility!

128

Notice verses 47 & 48 of Luke 12. We read that the servant who knew not his Lord's will and did not prepare shall be beaten with **few** stripes, but the servant which **knew** His Lord's will, but prepared not SHALL BE BEATEN WITH **many** stripes. "For unto whomsoever much is **given,** of him shall much **be required.**" The stripes here are not literal but figurative, and refer to the **time of tribulation** coming on the earth. Just what these "stripes" will involve I do not know, but I surmise that they refer to the buffeting by trying and difficult circumstances during the tribulation through **lack** of the complete protection and guidance of the Lord. They will be the natural consequence of a failure to prepare.

PROPHECIES:

PREPARE YE, PREPARE YE, SAITH THE LORD, FOR IT IS THE DAY OF THE LORD'S PREPARATION. FOR I WOULD HAVE MY PEOPLE PREPARE THEMSELVES FOR THAT WHICH IS COMING, SAITH THE LORD. FOR DOES A MAN GO INTO BATTLE WITHOUT PREPARATION? DOES AN ATHLETE ENGAGE IN A CONTEST WITHOUT TRAINING? I SAY UNTO YOU, IF YOU DO NOT LET ME PREPARE YOU FOR THAT WHICH IS COMING YOU WILL SURELY NOT BE ABLE TO STAND.

BUT HOW SHALL WE BE PREPARED, YOU ASK? **LET ME DO A WORK IN YOUR LIFE WHICH HAS NEVER BEEN DONE BEFORE,** FOR I AM ABLE SAITH GOD, TO TAKE THEE UNTO MYSELF AND PREPARE THEE AS A VESSEL WHICH SHALL BE USED OF ME AND WHICH SHALL SHOW FORTH MY GLORY. BUT FIRST YOU MUST BE WILLING. YOU MUST BE WILLING TO SUBMIT YOURSELVES TO ME IN EVERYTHING, YEA IN EVERY DETAIL OF THY LIFE. FOR I WILL TAKE YOU AND REMOULD YOU AND MAKE YOU A FIT VESSEL TO CONTAIN THAT WHICH IS NECESSARY TO WITHSTAND IN THIS EVIL DAY ALL OF THE ONSLAUGHTS OF THE ENEMY. THEREFORE MY PEOPLE, LET ME PREPARE YOU SAITH THE LORD. ...

AND IF THY HEART IS SET UPON ME TO DO MY WILL, I CERTAINLY WILL TEACH YOU MY WAYS, SAITH THE LORD. BUT **THERE MUST BE NO MIXTURE IN YOUR LIFE,** SAITH THE LORD, FOR IF YOUR HEART IS NOT SET UPON ME TO

KNOW MY TRUTH, AND TO DO MY WILL, YOU VERILY SHALL BE DECEIVED. FOR NONE SHALL BE ABLE TO STAND IN THIS DAY, EXCEPT THOSE I HAVE ESPECIALLY PREPARED. SO PREPARE, MY PEOPLE; I SAY AGAIN PREPARE! CAST ALL OTHER THINGS ASIDE AS NOTHING IN COMPARISON WITH THE ONE SUPREME GOAL OF SEEKING THY GOD, AND SEPARATING THYSELF UNTO HIM ... FOR IF YOU WILL NOT DO THIS YOU WILL NOT BE ABLE TO STAND, SAITH THE LORD. AND NOW, WHAT MUST YOU DO TO BECOME A VESSEL UNTO THE LORD? FIRST THERE MUST BE **A COM-PLETE EMPTYING OF ONESELF.** I WILL NOT ALLOW A MIX-TURE IN THAT WHICH I AM WORKING: IT MUST BE ALL OF ME AND NONE OF THYSELF. I CANNOT USE VESSELS IN THIS DAY WHO ARE EVEN A LITTLE BIT FILLED WITH THEIR OWN DESIRES, AND PLANS, AND SELFISH WAYS. THERE MUST BE A COMPLETE EMPTYING OF SELF, AND THEN ONLY CAN I FILL WITH THAT WHICH WILL BRING HONOR UNTO MYSELF, WHICH IS NOT A MIXTURE BUT THAT WHICH IS PURE AND TRUE. SO I WOULD HAVE THEE EMPTY THY-SELF COMPLETELY, AND LET ME FILL YOU SAITH THE LORD.

AND THEN FURTHER I WOULD HAVE YOU **MAKE THYSELF CONTINUALLY AVAILABLE FOR MY CLEANSINGS,** THAT I MAY REMOVE ANY DEPOSITS OR ACCUMULATION OF DE-BRIS WHICH MIGHT BE IN THY VESSEL. FOR I SAY, THE ENEMY IS ALWAYS READY TO SLIP THINGS IN ON THE SLY, AND CONTAMINATE THAT WHICH I AM PUTTING WITHIN YOU. THEREFORE YOU MUST CONSTANTLY SEARCH THINE OWN HEART THAT THOSE DEPOSITS WHICH HAVE RESULTED FROM SATAN'S DECEPTION BE REMOVED FROM THY VES-SEL, EVEN SO SHALL YE BE CLEAN AND PURE BEFORE ME, SAITH THE LORD.

EVEN SO AM I LOOKING ACROSS THE LAND SEEKING FOR VESSELS. SO MANY WANT TO BE INSTRUMENTS, BUT THEY ARE UNWILLING FIRST TO BECOME PREPARED VESSELS. AND BECAUSE OF THEIR UNWILLINGNESS TO YIELD THEM-SELVES WHOLLY UNTO ME, I CAN USE THEM VERY LITTLE, SAITH THE LORD. THE LAND IS FULL OF UNPREPARED VES-SELS WHO WANT TO BE INSTRUMENTS, BUT SO FEW WHO ARE WILLING TO BECOME VESSELS PREPARED, SAITH THE

LORD. SO CONTINUE TO SEEK ME, THAT I MAY REVEAL MY-
SELF UNTO YOU. AND **THINK NOT THAT YOU CAN BECOME
A MIGHTY INSTRUMENT, UNTIL FIRST I HAVE PREPARED YOU
AS A VESSEL.**

SO MY PEOPLE HEAR MY WORD, IF YOUR SPIRITUAL VISION
WOULD BE SOUND, AND THY WHOLE LIFE FLOODED WITH
THE LIGHT OF SPIRITUAL UNDERSTANDING AND PERCEP-
TION, LET ME CONTINUE TO DEAL WITH THEE CONCERN-
ING THY WILLINGNESS TO RECEIVE MY TRUTH. FOR MANY
THERE ARE WHO ARE WILLING TO RECEIVE SOME TRUTH,
AND THE LIGHT OF MY SPIRIT IS ABLE TO MAKE THAT TRUTH
REAL TO THEM, BUT THEN THEY HARDEN THEIR WILL AS
THEY BEGIN TO PERCEIVE HOW THEIR OWN DESIRES AND
SELF INTERESTS WILL BE AFFECTED. THEY ARE NOT WILL-
ING TO RECEIVE MORE LIGHT AND UNDERSTANDING, AND
THEIR SPIRITUAL VISION REMAINS DEFECTIVE. THE EYES
OF THEIR UNDERSTANDING ARE NOT FUNCTIONING IN COM-
PLETE SOUNDNESS. THEREFORE THEY ARE WALKING
PARTLY IN LIGHT AND PARTLY IN DARKNESS, AND THE LIGHT
WHICH THEY HAVE IS NOT SUFFICIENT TO LEAD THEM INTO
THAT PLACE OF COMPLETE VICTORY IN ME. THEIR SPIR-
ITUAL LIFE IS HAMPERED BECAUSE THERE IS NO COMPLETE
SOUNDNESS IN THEIR SPIRITUAL VISION.

WILL YE NOT HEAR MY PEOPLE, AND PRAY THAT THINE OWN
DESIRES WILL BE SO COMPLETELY YIELDED UNTO ME, THINE
OWN WILL SO COMPLETELY UNDER MY CONTROL, THAT
NOTHING SHALL KEEP YOU FROM GOING ON IN MY TRUTH.
**CONSIDER NOT THAT WHICH WILL RESULT IN THE EYES OF
MEN**; NEITHER HOW WHAT YOU BELIEVE WILL AFFECT THOSE
AROUND YOU, BUT KEEP YOUR HEART AND YOUR ATTEN-
TION CENTERED UPON ME, FOR I WILL NOT LET ANYTHING
HAPPEN TO THEE THAT IS NOT FOR THINE OWN GOOD, BUT
**I WILL SURELY KEEP YOU IN THAT WHICH WILL BRING THEE
FORTH IN MY PERFECT IMAGE AND LIKENESS.** FEAR NOT, I
SAY, FOR FEAR OF WHAT MEN MAY THINK IS THAT WHICH
ROBS YOU OF RECEIVING THE CONTINUOUS LIGHT AND
REVELATION OF MY SPIRIT. FOR FEARING FOR THINE OWN
REPUTATION IN THE SIGHT OF MEN, THOU DOST GIVE MORE
CONSIDERATION TO THINE OWN DESIRES AND THINE OWN
FLESH THAN TO THE LOVE OF THY GOD, AND IN DOING SO

THOU DOST SET THY WILL AGAINST HIS FURTHER LIGHT AND TRUTH. THEREFORE THY SPIRITUAL VISION REMAINS UNSOUND AND THY LIGHT IS TURNED TO DARKNESS.

PROPHECY BY KENNETH COPELAND DURING THE TEXAS SOUTH WEST BELIEVERS' CONVENTION – mid 1980s – at Fort Worth.

I am the great I Am, saith the Lord. My day and My hour has come. When My day and My hour came to be baptized in water, no man could stop me. When My hour came to be born in a manger, no devil could stop Me. When My hour came, Herod and all of his troops could not stop what was happening in the earth. It is no different now. I have chosen this hour and I have chosen this generation to be the generation that shall stand in great light and in great power. And while the devil creates a whirlwind here and a whirlwind there, and a storm here and a storm there, they will not have any impact or any effect on My plan and what I am doing with this army that I am building.

There's **a number in this army that have been training for years.** A number of you that have been training and you have been involved in small skirmishes here and there and the other place, and some of you feel as though you are battle scarred veterans. Oh, you have no concept of the victory that is in store for you. You have in your wildest dreams **no concept of what I'm going to allow to come to you in victory over darkness and over sin and over sickness and over demons and over fear.** As in the days of My earthly ministry when there were men that came back to me and said, **"Lord even the devils are subject to us in Your name,"** I said, **"Rejoice for your names are written in the Lamb's Book of Life."** Even the great things that they saw will only be child's play compared to the miraculous that shall occur in these days and has even already begun and is in its light stages now...

It's already happening. I'm uncovering revelation after revelation. **For these are the days of the greatest revelation of all...**

APPENDIX B

AUSTRALIAN PROPHECIES

SELECTED PROPHECIES FROM THE MINISTRY OF FULL SALVATION FELLOWSHIP

Introduction

The extracts presented below were prophesied by various members of the Fellowship during 1982-83 and without any prior knowledge of the American prophecies which were discovered in late 1983.

PROPHECY: Peter

THUS SAITH THE LORD—I THE LORD THY GOD AM A HOLY GOD AND A JEALOUS GOD AND IT IS NOT MY WILL THAT MY PEOPLE SHOULD BE INVADED AND THEIR LIVES INTRUDED UPON BY THOSE THINGS WHICH WOULD LEAD THEM TO DESTRUCTION. MY PEOPLE ARE A HOLY PEOPLE. YOU ARE INDEED A ROYAL PRIESTHOOD AND A HOLY NATION. I WOULD HAVE YOU RESPECT THAT YOU ARE HOLY, I WOULD HAVE YOU KNOW IT, AND FEEL IT AND EXPERIENCE IT. I HAVE SEPARATED YOU FROM THE WORLD TO SERVE ME. FOLLOW THE LEADING OF MY SPIRIT; I HAVE SEPARATED YOU UNTO MYSELF. I INDEED AM THE POTTER AND YOU ARE THE CLAY AND I AM MOULDING YOU. AND YOU SHALL BE MOULDED INTO VESSELS OF HONOUR IN MY FATHER'S HOUSE—SAITH THE LORD.

PROPHECY: Dorian

PREPARE YOURSELVES, MAKE READY SAYS THE LORD, BECAUSE INDEED THE TIME HAS COME, AND IS NOW AT HAND FOR MY RETURN. I AM COMING AND BEHOLD I AM COMING QUICKLY SAYS THE LORD. I AM COMING FOR MY BRIDE, AND I WOULD SAY UNTO MY BRIDE, I WOULD SAY, MAKE

YOURSELVES READY, CLOTHE YOURSELF IN WHITE GAR-
MENTS, WHICH IS THE RIGHTEOUSNESS OF THE SAINTS,
AND CLOTHE YOURSELVES EVEN IN MY RIGHTEOUSNESS
SAITH THE LORD AND EQUIP YOURSELF WITH THE WHOLE
ARMOUR OF GOD THAT YOU MIGHT BE ABLE TO STAND IN
THE EVIL DAY, THAT YOU MIGHT BE ABLE TO STAND IN THE
DAYS THAT COME AHEAD, THAT ARE COMING. AND I WOULD
SAY UNTO YOU, **FEED UPON MY WORD** AND BUILD YOUR-
SELF UP IN MY WORD. AND INCREASE STRENGTH AND PUT
ON STRENGTH AND PUT ON MIGHT, EVEN MY MIGHT, THAT
YOU MIGHT BE STRONG IN MY POWER (AND NOT IN YOUR
OWN, NOT IN THE ARM OF THE FLESH, IN YOUR OWN POWER)
BUT IN MY POWER AND IN THE STRENGTH OF MY WORD,
FOR THE DAYS ARE COMING SAYS THE LORD WHEN DIS-
TRESS SHALL BE UPON MANY AND THERE SHALL BE AF-
FLICTION AND THERE SHALL BE TROUBLE AND IT HAS EVEN
BEGUN AND THE TIME SHALL BECOME HARD SAYS THE
LORD. AND I WOULD SAY PREPARE YOURSELVES EVEN NOW
AND MAKE READY FOR MY COMING THAT YOU BE CLOTHED
AND NOT WALK NAKED SAYS THE LORD. BUT YOU SHOULD
BE CLOTHED IN THE RIGHTEOUSNESS, EVEN IN MY RIGHT-
EOUSNESS, THAT YOU SHOULD BE PREPARED AT MY COM-
ING FOR THAT DAY. YOU ARE NOT IN DARKNESS THAT THEY
SHOULD OVERTAKE YOU AS A THIEF, BECAUSE YOU HAVE
BEEN WARNED AND YOU KNOW THAT I AM COMING FOR MY
PRECIOUS BRIDE. I LOVE YOU SO MUCH AND I WOULD HAVE
YOU BE READY FOR ME WHEN I COME. SO PREPARE YOUR-
SELF, BUILD YOURSELF UP. STRENGTHEN YOURSELF IN MY
WORD AND PUT ON THE RIGHTEOUSNESS, EVEN MY RIGHT-
EOUSNESS, THAT YOU SHOULD WALK IN THE LIGHT AND NOT
IN DARKNESS. AND MY BLOOD SHALL CLEANSE YOU OF
EVERY SIN AND I SHALL COME AND TAKE YOU UNTO MY-
SELF AND YOU SHALL BE WITH ME AND I SHALL LOVE YOU
AND I SHALL FELLOWSHIP WITH YOU AND YOU SHALL REIGN
WITH ME. FOR I AM YOUR GOD AND I AM YOUR HUSBAND
SAYS THE LORD FOR YOU ARE MY BRIDE AND I WILL CHER-
ISH YOU EVEN THOUGH I CHERISH YOU NOW. YOU WILL BE
WITH ME AND I SHALL HONOUR YOU AND YOU SHALL HON-
OUR ME AND WE SHALL HAVE SWEET FELLOWSHIP TO-
GETHER FOR I LOVE YOU SO MUCH. YOU ARE PRECIOUS IN
MY SIGHT, **YOU ARE A PRECIOUS JEWEL,** SAITH THE LORD,
TO ME, AND I LOVE YOU SAITH THE LORD.

135

PROPHECY: Ethel

...POLISHING WOOD AS A POLISHED SHAFT. I WILL NOT BE
SATISFIED UNTIL YOU ARE SO SMOOTH, THAT WHEN I SHOOT
YOU, YOU WILL SERVE THE PURPOSE FOR WHAT YOUR LIFE
IS FOR. I LOVE YOU AND AS I HAVE ALREADY SAID, **I AM A
HOLY GOD AND MY CHILDREN ARE TO BE HOLY AND PER-
FECT.** AT PRESENT I AM HIDING YOU IN MY QUIVER AND I
TAKE YOU OUT AND I POLISH YOU BECAUSE YOU ARE MY
PEOPLE AND YOU WILL PENETRATE INTO THAT DARKNESS
AND EACH TIME I USE YOU, YOU WILL BE USED FOR MY
GLORY. SO FEAR NOT WHEN I DEAL HEAVILY WITH YOU BE-
CAUSE I AM GENTLE AND WHAT I DO IS GOOD. YOU ARE MY
CHILDREN AND **I DECLARE NOW BE YE HOLY, EVEN AS I AM
HOLY, BE YE PERFECT, EVEN AS I AM PERFECT,** AND THAT IS
WHAT I AM DOING WITH YOUR LIVES NOW—TO THE GLORY
OF MY OWN SON JESUS.

PROPHECY: Peter

I THE LORD THY GOD AM A JEALOUS GOD AND VISIT THE
SINS OF THE FATHERS UPON THE CHILDREN EVEN UNTO
THE THIRD AND FOURTH GENERATION OF THEM THAT HATE
ME AND I SHOW MERCY AND PARDON TO THOSE WHO LOVE
ME AND KEEP MY COMMANDMENTS. AND I AM A HOLY GOD
AND I SEPARATE BEFORE MYSELF A PEOPLE, A PEOPLE TO
KNOW THAT I AM HOLY; AND THAT I AM A GOD OF POWER
AND A GOD OF JUDGEMENT AND A GOD OF WAR AND I AM A
GOD OF MERCY, SLOW TO ANGER, MERCIFUL EVEN BEYOND
THE DEPTHS OF THE OCEANS. (IT IS) MY PURPOSE TO
GATHER UNTO MYSELF A PEOPLE THAT SHALL BE HOLY, THE
REDEEMED OF THE LORD. AND THEIR BANNER SHALL BE
THE BANNER OF THE LORD AND THEIR WAR SHALL BE THE
WAR OF THE LORD AND THEIR POWER SHALL BE THE POWER
OF THE LORD, AND THEY SHALL OVERCOME ALL THEIR EN-
EMIES AND COME TO THEIR PLACE WHERE THEY SHALL
FIND REST AND PEACE. THEY SHALL COME TO THEIR PLACE
WHICH IS MY SABBATH. EVEN MORE, THEY SHALL FIND THAT
SABBATH REST IN ALL ITS MEANING, FOR I HAVE SEPARATED
THEM AND CALLED THEM UNTO MYSELF AS MY HOLY PEO-
PLE AND THERE SHALL NO POLLUTED THING GROW
AMONGST THEM—ALL THAT IS POLLUTED AND UNCLEAN

SHALL NOT BE FOUND AMONGST THEM. AND I THE LORD AM DOING THIS, FOR MY GLORY AND FOR MY NAME'S SAKE. THEREFORE COME TO ME WITH FAITH AND WITH COURAGE. STAND FIRM, HOLD FAST THAT WHICH IS GOOD, AND YOU SHALL SEE THE DAY OF THE LORD REVEALED, AND MY GREAT SALVATION.

PROPHECY: Ethel

MY PEOPLE I TELL YOU, GO OUT AND SOUND THE ALARM, LET THE TRUMPETS BLOW AND LET ALL MY PEOPLE COME OUT FROM THEIR TRIBES. LET THEM MOVE IN FROM THEIR TRIBES AND COME TOGETHER TO THE HEAVENLY TENT OF MEETING AND THAT IS WHERE I WANT YOU ALL TOGETHER IN THE SPIRIT, AND REMEMBER, THAT MY LIGHT HAS SHONE UPON YOU. ARISE BECAUSE MY LIGHT HAS SHONE UPON YOU, AND BE READY, BECAUSE **I AM GOING TO DO A NEW THING** AND WHEN YOU ARE GATHERED TOGETHER, ALL TO-GETHER IN ONE GROUP, MY CHURCH, OUT OF THE TRIBES, COME TOGETHER TO THIS TENT OF MEETING, YOU BE READY. BE PREPARED, BECAUSE YOU ARE GOING TO FOL-LOW THE STANDARD OF MY SON. BE PREPARED TO FOL-LOW HIM, BECAUSE **I AM DOING A NEW THING IN THIS EARTH**, AND YOU, MY PEOPLE, I AM GOING TO USE TO DO IT, SO BE PREPARED TO COME, AND FOLLOW MY SON, AND FEAR NOT, BECAUSE MY GLORY IS SHINING ON YOU.

RISE UP AND LOOK, SEE THE DARKNESS THAT IS ON THE EARTH, SEE THE GREAT DARKNESS THAT IS ALL OVER THE PEOPLE, BUT MY LIGHT HAS SHONE UPON YOU, AND MY GLORY IS RESTING UPON YOU, BECAUSE YOU ARE MY PEO-PLE, AND I AM YOUR GOD, SAITH THE LORD.

YEA, SAITH THE LORD, YOU LOOK ABOUT YOU, AND SEE A SEETHING LIKE A POT BUBBLING, AND YOU SAY THAT I THE LORD AM NOT DOING ANYTHING, BUT I THE LORD THY GOD AM LIGHTING FIRES THROUGHOUT THE WHOLE UNIVERSE, AND I WILL BLOW UPON THEM. THEY ARE BECOMING MIGHTY FLAMES, AND EVIL MEN SHALL SAY IN THEIR HEARTS "LET US DESTROY THEM. LET US PUT THEM FAR FROM US," AND THEY LOOK FOR THEM AND THEY SHALL BE GONE.

Later prophecies from 1986 onwards:

PROPHECY: Shirley

GLORIFY MY NAME, GLORIFY IT AND AGAIN I SAY GLORIFY, GLORIFY, EXALT MY NAME, RAISE IT HIGH ABOVE THE HEAVENS. THIS NAME HAS ALL POWER AND ALL THE AUTHORITY ON HEAVEN AND EARTH. THIS IS NOT JUST WORDS MY CHILDREN. THIS HAS TRUE MEANING. MY NAME HAS ALL POWER, MY NAME IS ALL AUTHORITY. LET THE WORLD KNOW ABOUT IT, LET THE WORLD KNOW MY NAME AND LET IT FEEL MY POWER. LET IT FEEL MY AUTHORITY. LET IT FLOW, LET IT FLOW THROUGH YOU NOW, NOW THIS VERY MINUTE. THE TIME IS SHORT. THE HOUR HAS COME, LET THIS AUTHORITY AND POWER BE KNOWN NOW, NOW: NOW AND AGAIN I SAY NOW. THIS IS THE APPOINTED TIME, EXALT MY NAME, NEVER STOP EXALTING ME, NEVER STOP GLORIFYING ME AND I WILL BLESS YOU BEYOND ALL MEASURE.

PROPHECY: Don

I WANT TO GIVE YOU MY LOVE, MY CHILDREN. I WANT TO SURROUND YOU WITH MY ARMS AND PROTECT YOU AND KEEP YOU. I WILL PULL YOU, **I WILL PULL YOU OUT OF BONDAGE. I WILL PULL YOU OUT OF THE MUD AND I WILL PULL YOU OUT OF THE DEEP MIRE AND I SHALL WASH YOU.** I SHALL WASH YOU CLEAN AND I SHALL SET YOUR FEET UPON THE ROCK, THE ROCK OF MY SON, JESUS CHRIST, AND I SHALL SET YOU UPON THAT ROCK AND **NOTHING** SHALL MOVE YOU. YOU SHALL BE **IMMOVABLE** AND I SHALL CALL YOU MY PEOPLE AND I SHALL PUT MY NAME IN YOU, AND YOU SHALL STAND. YOU SHALL STAND AGAINST THE GATES OF HELL EVEN, FOR I HAVE PUT MY ARM AROUND YOU. WITH MY RIGHT ARM I WILL LIFT YOU UP AND I WILL STRENGTHEN YOU AND I WILL **STRENGTHEN** YOU, AND IT IS MY STRENGTH THAT WILL BE IN YOU AND YOU WILL BE MY PEOPLE AND I WILL BE YOUR GOD, JUST AS I WAS THE GOD OF ABRAHAM AND THE GOD OF MOSES.

PROPHECY: Peter   30th March 1986
(1st Prophet)

I AM THE RESURRECTION AND THE LIFE SAITH THE LORD

138

AND WHOEVER BELIEVES IN ME SHALL LIVE, AND THE LIFE THAT I HAVE PREPARED FOR MY PEOPLE IS THE LIFE OF CHRIST HIMSELF.

I WOULD HAVE MY PEOPLE TRANSFORMED BY THE RENEW-ING OF THEIR MINDS. I WOULD HAVE THEM CONFORMED TO THE IMAGE OF THE SON OF GOD AND I WOULD HAVE MY PEOPLE KNOW THAT TO BE CONFORMED TO THE IMAGE OF THE SON OF GOD IS INDEED A MIGHTY TRANSFORMATION. A TRANSFORMATION IS NECESSARY THAT IS FAR GREATER THAN YOU WOULD EVER IMAGINE. THE TRANSFORMATION THAT IS NECESSARY BEGINS FROM DEEP WITHIN YOU. IT REQUIRES THE **CLEANSING OF YOUR SOUL**. IT REQUIRES THE **FULLNESS OF MY SPIRIT**. IT REQUIRES THE **RENEWING OF YOUR MIND**. IT REQUIRES THE **HEALING OF YOUR BODY**. IT REQUIRES A **TOTAL RESTORATION** OF EVERY PART OF YOUR BEING. IT REQUIRES THAT YOU BE **STRONG IN MY SPIRIT**. IT REQUIRES THAT YOU **SHED ALL THAT IS OF THIS WORLD**; THAT YOU **PUT TO DEATH THE THINGS OF THE FLESH** IN YOUR LIFE. IT REQUIRES THAT YOU **BE CRUCIFIED WITH THE SON OF GOD**; THAT YOU **SHARE IN THE FELLOW-SHIP OF HIS SUFFERINGS**—AND ONLY THEN CAN YOU SAY THAT YOU ARE CONFORMED TO HIS IMAGE. ONLY THEN CAN YOU SAY THAT YOU HAVE BEEN TRANSFORMED, THAT YOUR MIND IS THE MIND OF CHRIST.

MY PEOPLE, **YOU KNOW THERE IS MUCH THAT IS TO BE PUT TO DEATH IN YOUR LIVES, MUCH THAT IS UNWORTHY OF THE SON OF GOD.** ARE YOU PREPARED TO BE CRUCI-FIED WITH HIM? YOU CANNOT KNOW THE POWER OF HIS RESURRECTION UNTIL YOU HAVE SHARED IN THE FEL-LOWSHIP OF HIS SUFFERINGS. AND YET I CAN PROMISE YOU THAT IN THE MIDST OF THAT WALK, ALTHOUGH YOU SHALL KNOW WHAT IT IS TO BE GRIEVED IN YOUR SPIRIT, TO WEEP FOR THOSE WHO ARE REBELLIOUS, TO WEEP FOR THOSE WHO CONTINUE ON THE ROAD TO THE LAKE OF FIRE—THE BROAD ROAD THAT LEADS TO THEIR DESTRUCTION—YET IN THE MIDST OF ALL THAT YOU WILL KNOW THE JOY THAT IS SUPPLIED TO YOU FROM THE THRONE OF GOD. YOU WILL KNOW THE PEACE THAT TRULY DOES PASS UNDER-STANDING AND MY JOY SHALL FLOW IN YOU AND THROUGH YOU AND SUSTAIN YOU, FOR IN MY JOY SHALL BE YOUR

STRENGTH AND YOU WILL BE ENABLED TO OVERCOME EVERY OBSTACLE.

Don
(2nd Prophet)

... **YOU** ARE MY CRAFTSMANSHIP. I HAVE LABOURED IN LOVE OVER YOU. I HAVE LABOURED IN LOVE TO BRING YOU FORTH INTO THAT GLORY THAT I ORDAINED. EVEN BEFORE THE EARTH WAS MADE, I LOVED YOU AND I CALLED YOU, AND NOW I AM BRINGING YOU FORTH LIKE A NEW DAY. I WILL PUT A NEW SONG IN YOUR MOUTH, EVEN PRAISE TO MY NAME. AND I WANT YOU TO KNOW THAT THROUGH ME AND THROUGH OBEDIENCE TO ME, TO MY WORD, YOU WILL AT-TAIN THE FULFILMENT OF **ALL** YOUR GLORY IN THIS LIFE HERE. YOU SHALL ATTAIN FULFILMENT; YOU SHALL ATTAIN FULFILMENT TO YOUR HEART'S JOY; SUCH JOY YOU CAN NEVER COMPREHEND, FOR I AM BRINGING YOU FORTH AS MY CRAFTSMANSHIP. LIKE THE CRAFTSMAN WHO SPENDS HOURS LABOURING OVER HIS WORK TO PERFECT IT IN BEAUTY, SO AM I LABOURING OVER YOU HERE, NOW, THROUGH THIS MINISTRY WHICH I HAVE ORDAINED; THIS MINISTRY WHICH I HAVE RAISED UP. NOW MY CHILDREN **YOU SHALL COME FORTH AS A BEAUTIFUL JEWEL**, A BEAUTIFUL CAMEO, THAT WILL REFLECT MY LOVE TO ALL THE NATIONS OF THE EARTH AND **YOU SHALL BE CALLED THE BRIDE OF CHRIST.** YOU SHALL BE ARRAYED IN ALL THE BEAUTY OF A VIRGIN BRIDE; FOR THAT IS MY HANDIWORK FOR YOU THIS DAY AND I LABOUR OVER YOU IN LOVE—DELICATELY I HAVE FASHIONED YOU.

THIS IS THE WORD OF YOUR FATHER; HEAR IT AND BE OBE-DIENT TO IT AND YOU SHALL KNOW MY LOVE IN ALL ITS FULLNESS.

PROPHECY: Peter   Sunday, 21st October 1990

THUS SAYS THE LORD:

MY SPIRIT HOVERS OVER MY CREATION TO BRING LIFE, AND EVEN THOUGH THE CREATION IS DEFILED, POLLUTED WITH SIN AND DEATH, DESTROYED AND LAID WASTE BY THE

ABUSE OF MANKIND, YET DOES MY SPIRIT HOVER OVER THIS CREATION. MY SPIRIT BRINGS LIFE TO THE DEAD. MY SPIRIT WILL DRAW TOGETHER THE BONES OF ISRAEL AND BREATHE THE LIFE OF CHRIST INTO THOSE BONES, AND IT (THEY) SHALL STAND FLESHED AND STRONG AND BECOME A MIGHTY ARMY. (Gen. 1:2; Isa. 31:5; Isa. 24:3-6; Rom. 8:11; Ezek. 37:1-14; Rom. 8:20-21; Rom. 5:12).

MY SPIRIT SWEEPS OVER THE SOULS OF MY CHILDREN TO CLEANSE AND TO PURIFY, FOR MY SPIRIT IS A REFINING SPIRIT AND WILL BURN THE DROSS AND THE UGLY FROM MY CREATION. AND YET MY SPIRIT WILL CALL AND WILL ALIGHT ON THOSE WHO DO NOT YET KNOW ME, FOR MANY ARE YET TO BE CALLED AND COME INTO MY BLESSING. FROM EVERY TRIBE AND TONGUE AND NATION WILL I CALL THE HARVEST UNTO MYSELF. (1 Cor. 3:12-13; 2 Peter 3:7,10; Joel 2:28-32; Rev. 7:9; Matt. 9:37-38).

AND WHEN MANKIND HAS DONE WITH HIS DESTRUCTIVE WAYS AND BROUGHT THE EARTH TO A STANDSTILL, EVEN THEN AT THE SOUND OF THE TRUMPET WILL THE DEAD IN CHRIST RISE TO BE CAUGHT UP, TOGETHER WITH THOSE WHO ARE ALIVE. MY SPIRIT SHALL DO IT. (Isa. 24:20; 1 Thess. 4:16-17; 1 Cor. 15:51-52).

AND THEN SHALL MY SPIRIT RESTORE THE EARTH AND ALL THAT I HAVE CREATED. THE UNCLEAN SPIRIT SHALL BE RE-MOVED FROM THE LAND AND THERE WILL BE RIVERS OF LIVING WATER, NOT ONLY FLOWING FROM THE BELLIES OF MY PEOPLE, BUT ACROSS THE NATIONS... AND THE DESERTS SHALL SPRING TO LIFE AND ALL CREATION SHALL REJOICE AT THE REVEALING OF THE CHILDREN OF GOD. THE BOND-AGE TO DECAY SHALL BE FINISHED AND DEATH SHALL HAVE NO MORE DOMINION. (Rev. 21:1-4; Isa. 34:16-35:10; Zech. 13:2; John 7:37-39; Isa. 44:3; Joel 2:28; Isa. 35:1; Rom. 8:19,21; Isa. 25:7-8; 1 Cor. 15:54-57; Rom. 6:9; Rom. 6:14; Rev. 1:18).

THE FLOODS WILL CLAP THEIR HANDS AND THE HILLS SHALL REJOICE AT THE GLORY OF THE LORD AND THE MOUNTAINS SHALL BE MADE LOW AND THE LOW PLACES

SHALL BE RAISED AND THE GLORY OF THE LORD SHALL BE REVEALED IN ALL THE EARTH AND (IT) SHALL PRAISE MY HOLY NAME. (Ps. 98:8; Isa. 40:4-5; Luke 3:5-6; Ps. 150:6).

AND THE RESTORATION SHALL BE COMPLETE, FOR I THE LORD HAVE SPOKEN IT. (Rev. 21:1-22:5; Isa. 25:8).

PROPHECY: Peter

Sunday, 11th November 1990—continued from 21st October 1990

SO THEN YIELD TO MY SPIRIT AS IT MOVES ACROSS THE EARTH, AND AS MY SPIRIT MINISTERS TO YOU, BE FULLY PART OF MY GREAT RESTORATION. HUNGER AND THIRST TO BE A PART OF IT. (Heb. 2:3; Matt. 5:6).

DO NOT SAY TO MY SPIRIT–"NO",–BUT SUBMIT TO HIM; AL-LOW HIM TO MINISTER TO YOUR DEEPEST NEEDS. DO NOT PUT IT OFF FOR ANOTHER TIME—FOR THERE MAY NOT BE ANOTHER TIME, FOR YOU. RECEIVE NOW, ALL THAT MY SPIRIT HAS FOR YOU AND BE GRATEFUL. PRAISE THE LORD YOUR GOD FOR HIS PROVISION FOR YOU AND SEEK ALL THAT HE HAS FOR YOU, TODAY. (Jonah 1:1-3; James 4:7; Luke 4:17-21; Luke 12:20; Rom. 13:11; 2 Cor. 6:2; Ps. 103:1-5; Luke 11:9-10).

ONLY AS YOU FLOW WITH MY SPIRIT CAN YOU BELONG TO MY MIGHTY PURPOSES, AND RECEIVE THE INHERITANCE THAT I HAVE STORED UP FOR YOU IN HEAVEN. (Rom. 8:14; 1 Peter 1:4)

APPENDIX C

CONTINENTAL PROPHECY

FROM THE 1975 CONTINENTAL CONFERENCE ROME—ITALY

"During the Continental Conference, the Lord spoke through Prophecy about what He is doing in the world today and how His people· should respond. The following are excerpts from prophecies given at the general sessions of the conference. They should be understood not as an isolated word but as part of the larger work the Lord was doing at the conference. Through His Word, the Lord steadies us in His love and prepares us for the challenges of the days ahead." **("New Covenant" Magazine August 1976).**

MY BELOVED, YOU MY PEOPLE WHO STAND BEFORE ME NOW: HEAR MY WORD. **I WILL SET MY HOUSE IN ORDER. I WILL PURIFY MY PEOPLE. I WILL PURIFY MY CHURCH.** I SHALL SET ASIDE THE DECEIVER, THE FALSE PROPHET, AND THE FALSE TEACHER. **I SHALL SET ASIDE ANYTHING AND ANYONE WHO STANDS IN THE WAY OF MY KINGDOM. ...**

THE LORD SAYS, I RAISE MY VOICE, BUT WHO LISTENS TO ME? I CRY OUT, BUT WHO HEEDS MY WORD? **THIS IS A TIME OF BUILDING UP AND OF WASTING AWAY.** THIS IS A TIME OF UNRAVELLING. THIS IS A TIME WHEN I ESTABLISH MY KINGDOM **AND EVERY OTHER KINGDOM COLLAPSES.** I RAISE MY VOICE TO WARN MY PEOPLE, AND WHO TAKES HEED? A CLOUD HANGS OVER YOU, A SHADOW ENVELOPS YOU. DO YOU NOT HEAR MY VOICE? THERE IS DARKNESS AROUND YOU.

ANYTHING THAT IS NOT BUILT BY MY HAND WILL BE WASHED AWAY. ANYTHING THAT DOES NOT COME FROM ME WILL NOT SURVIVE. I CRY OUT TO YOU. DO YOU HEAR MY VOICE? **I RAISE MY VOICE TO SAVE MY PEOPLE, AND THEY DON'T LISTEN. THIS IS A TIME OF BUILDING UP AND OF TEARING DOWN. I HAVE TO BUILD MY CHURCH. I HAVE TO PREVENT**

144

MY PEOPLE FROM BEING TORN DOWN. LET YOUR EARS BE OPEN; LET YOUR HEARTS BE RECEPTIVE. RECEIVE THE WORD THAT I BRING NOW. THIS IS AN IMPORTANT TIME FOR MY PEOPLE. THIS IS A DAY OF DECISION THAT CANNOT BE PASSED BY. I RAISE MY VOICE. I CALL FORTH MY PEOPLE. WHO WILL LISTEN TO ME? WHO WILL RESPOND TO MY CALL?

... I TELL YOU, MY PEOPLE, THERE ARE SOME HERE WHO NEED TO UNDERSTAND THIS: **WAYS YOU HAVE RESPONDED TO ME IN THE PAST, THAT HAVE SEEN YOU THROUGH AND BROUGHT YOU THUS FAR, WILL NO LONGER SEE YOU THROUGH. WHAT I CALL YOU TO IS SOMETHING NEW, SOMETHING TOTALLY NEW**; AND WHERE THERE IS RESISTANCE IN YOUR HEARTS AND IN YOUR GROUPS, LAY DOWN THAT RESISTANCE THAT I MIGHT BRING YOU FURTHER ALONG.

I SEE EACH ONE OF YOU WHERE YOU ARE. **I KNOW WHERE IT'S HARD FOR YOU TO CHANGE, AND I CANNOT PROMISE TO YOU THAT CHANGE WILL BE EASY, OR THAT IT WILL COME IMMEDIATELY. I CANNOT PROMISE THAT IT WON'T BE PAINFUL, FOR INDEED IT SHALL COST YOU,** BUT I CAN PROMISE YOU THIS: I SHALL BE WITH YOU ALWAYS AND THE PAIN IS NOTHING COMPARED TO WHAT I WILL GIVE YOU IN RETURN. WHAT YOU NEED TO LAY DOWN, AND WHAT YOU WILL GIVE UP, AND WHAT YOU THINK IT WILL COST YOU IS NOTHING COMPARED TO THE STRENGTH YOU WILL HAVE WHEN I AM FINISHED WITH YOU.

... THEREFORE, YOU CAN KNOW IN JOY THAT MY HOLY SPIRIT IS UPON YOU, AND THAT MY PRESENCE IS WITH YOU IN THE TIME OF TESTING THAT LIES AHEAD: FOR WHEN YOU ARE CALLED TO SUFFER IN THE DAYS TO COME, TO SPEND YOURSELVES IN THE DAYS TO COME, TO LAY DOWN YOUR LIVES, YOUR HOMES, YOUR MONEY—THERE ARE EVEN SOME AMONG YOU WHO WILL SHED YOUR BLOOD FOR MY NAME'S SAKE—WHEN THAT DAY COMES YOU WILL SAY THAT I SPOKE TO YOU ON THIS NIGHT AND SHOWED YOU MY PRESENCE AND MY POWER. THEREFORE, MY PEOPLE, KNOW THIS, THAT MY SPIRIT RESTS UPON EACH OF YOUR HEADS, AND I CALL YOU NOW TO RECEIVE PERSONALLY AND DEEPLY THE ANOINTING AND THE EMPOWERING TO RECEIVE THE WORD I HAVE SPOKEN TO YOU HERE TONIGHT, AND TO ACCOMPLISH IT ACCORDING TO MY WILL FOR YOU. ...

APPENDIX D

RESTORATION SCRIPTURES

1. "We (Christians)," Paul wrote, "ARE BEING CHANGED into His likeness (image) from glory into glory..." (2 Cor. 3:18).

2. **"LET US CLEANSE OURSELVES FROM ALL POLLUTION of flesh and of spirit, perfecting holiness (separation for God's purposes) in the fear of God." (2 Cor. 7:1).**

3. "You sinners cleanse your hands (from evil deeds) and PURIFY YOUR HEARTS, you that are double-minded (two-souled)". (James 4:8).

4. "If therefore anyone CLEANSES himself, he will be a sanctified vessel for honour ... Flee youthful lusts, and pursue righteousness, faith, love, peace with those who call on the Lord out of a PURE HEART." (2 Tim. 2:21-22).

5. "Beloved, now we are children of God and it has not yet been shown what we shall be. We know that when He (Jesus?) is manifested WE SHALL BE LIKE HIM, because we shall see Him as He is.

   And EVERYONE having this hope concerning Him PURIFIES HIMSELF as He is pure". (1 John 3:2-3).

6. "Many will be purged, purified (made white) and refined, but the wicked will act wickedly, and none of the wicked will understand—but those who have insight will understand." (Dan. 12:10 N.A.S. Bible).

7.   It is written of **John the Baptist** that:

...he came into all the district around the Jordan, preaching a baptism of repentance for forgiveness of sins; as it is written in the book of the words of Isaiah the prophet, "The voice of one crying in the wilderness,

'MAKE READY THE WAY OF THE LORD. MAKE HIS PATHS STRAIGHT. EVERY RAVINE SHALL BE FILLED UP, AND EVERY MOUNTAIN AND HILL SHALL BE BROUGHT LOW; AND THE CROOKED SHALL BECOME STRAIGHT, AND THE ROUGH ROADS SMOOTH; AND ALL FLESH SHALL SEE THE SALVATION OF GOD.'"

He therefore said to the multitudes who were going out to be baptized by him, "You brood of vipers, who warned you to flee from the wrath to come?

"Therefore bring forth fruits in keeping with your repentance, and do not begin to say to yourselves, 'We have Abraham for our father,' for I say to you that God is able from these stones to raise up children to Abraham.

"And also the axe is already laid at the root of the trees; every tree therefore that does not bear good fruit is cut down and thrown into the fire." (Luke 3:4-9)

Please note, an explanation in full of these scriptures is made in **"Guidance for Those Receiving Deliverance."**

APPENDIX E

BODY AND BRIDE OF CHRIST

"But the Spirit explicitly says that in later times some will fall away from the faith, paying attention to deceitful spirits and doctrines of demons." (1 Timothy 4:1)

Here we provide for your study a comparison between the **Body of Christ** through history and the END-TIME **Bride of Christ.**

The Bible truth that God elects people to eternal life and none shall pluck those so chosen out of His hand has somehow led to the pernicious doctrine of "once saved always saved", mainly because Christians have failed to distinguish between 'saved' and 'elect'. **Once elect always elect does NOT mean once saved always saved.** Election is an eternal matter whereas salvation has a much broader meaning and may refer to only a temporal, earthly and very temporary condition, as the Israel that was saved from the Egyptians discovered to their cost in the wilderness. The letter to the Hebrews is a great help in understanding that a saved people are not necessarily elect. **It is how you finish the race that counts!** (1 Cor. 9:26-27).

Faith may lead to salvation TEMPORARILY, but Faith and **Obedience** lead to salvation ETERNALLY, which **Obedience** makes our election certain (2 Peter 1:10).

I believe it to be a most destructive error to teach that a conversion experience guarantees eternal life, **regardless of ensuing conduct,** although such a convert may be described as saved in the short term. By their fruits you shall know them.

BODY OF CHRIST	BRIDE OF CHRIST
1. 10 Virgins (Matt. 25:1-12).	5 Virgins
2. Various levels of oil.	Full of oil, trimmed lamps.
3. Souls are a mixture, i.e. Holy Spirit and religious spirits etc. (James 1:8, 3:8-12).	Fully filled with the Spirit (Eph. 5:18).
4. Half-ready and prone to play games of self-deception.	Serious about making themselves ready (Luke 9:23).
5. Spiritually asleep (Luke 22:46).	Watching and praying (Luke 21:36).
6. Saved by faith in the present NOW (TEMPORALLY) e.g. Israel in the wilderness (1 Cor. 10:1-13).	Elect and saved by faith temporally and PERMANENTLY because of God's secret decree (John 10:27-29).
7. May believe "Once saved always saved".	Believes salvation is for those faithful and obedient until death or Rapture (John 3:36).
8. Can presume unwisely upon conversion experience (salvation), past faith and Christ's Atonement (1 Cor. 10:-12).	Never stops changing into Christ likeness through the pursuit of holiness and inner cleansing (2 Cor. 3:18, 7:1).
9. May defect and fall from grace through partial commitment (Gal. 5:4).	Attain their goal (prize) because totally committed (Phil. 3:11-15).
10. Calls Jesus "Lord" (Matt. 7:21).	Calls Jesus "Lord" and DOES what He says (Matt. 7:21-27).
11. Growing in shallow, weedy and good soil (Mark 4:3-20).	Growing in good soil only and bears fruit.
12. Names are written in the Book of Life but can be blotted out! (Rev. 3:5).	Names STAY in the Book of Life (Rev. 3:5, 20:15).

APPENDIX F

FRUIT OF THE HOLY SPIRIT

GALATIANS 5:22-23	COLOSSIANS 3:12-16	2 CORINTHIANS 6:4-7
1. LOVE	LOVE	LOVE
2. JOY		
3. PEACE	PEACE	
4. PATIENCE	PATIENCE	PATIENCE
5. KINDNESS	KINDNESS ⁄	KINDNESS
6. GOODNESS		
7. FAITH(FULNESS)		
8. GENTLENESS	GENTLENESS	
9. SELF-CONTROL		
10.	(BOWELS OF) COMPASSION	
11.	HUMILITY	
12.	FORBEARANCE	
13.	FORGIVENESS	
14.	THANKFULNESS	
15.		ENDURANCE
16.		MORAL PURITY (INNOCENCE)
17.		KNOWLEDGE
18.	THE INDWELLING WORD OF CHRIST	THE WORD OF TRUTH
19.	WISDOM	
20.		THE POWER OF GOD

You should be able to find more fruit of the Holy Spirit in the Bible than those listed above, but this appendix will have served the Lord's purposes **if it expands your understanding beyond Galatians 5:22-23** into the fulness of the character of Jesus Christ, who is our beginning and our ending. (See also Isaiah 11:1-5, Romans 12:8-13).

APPENDIX G

THE PURSUIT OF PERFECTION

What does it mean for the Bride to make herself ready—to be without spot or wrinkle—or for every Christian to be cleansed, purified and conformed to the image of the Son of God, that is, perfect? Just look at those phrases (above) for a moment. Don't they just take your breath away? Do they give you a sense of despair because God's requirements from us are unattainable? **With men these aims ARE unattainable and impossible, but not with God.**

For centuries the Church has been alarmed at any notion of **"sinless perfectionism"** and has quite rightly underlined that at the Cross, Jesus the Son of God made an exchange with those who have put their trust in Him. **He gave them His perfection and took from them all their pollution.** By His blood sacrifice of Himself He obtained a pardon for all our sins, and this pardon becomes ours individually by repentance and faith in Him.

But now the NEW THING is unfolding and we need to look again at the Lord's command to be perfect. We discover from the Word of God that it has four (4) kinds of meaning in a Christian's life, as follows:

(i) Positional perfection (legal)

This is already possessed by every true believer in Christ—**"For by one offering he HAS PERFECTED FOREVER those who are being sanctified"** (Heb. 10:14). Other words often used to describe this LEGAL position of being perfected forever are **reconciled, forgiven, justified, righteous,** and as we have said, that means the perfection or righteousness of Christ Jesus is IMPUTED to us and so we are reckoned or accounted righteous or perfect LEGALLY, though we be far from righteous experientially.

(ii) Progressive or Relative perfection (changing present experience)

So-called because it has to do with our progressive Christian growth and sanctification now, in this life-time, and is often translated "mature"; e.g.:

"Let us therefore, as many **as be perfect...**
(Phil. 3:15, cf. 1 Cor. 2:6).

Its usual interpretation here is that of maturity, because it is often tied in with Christian character, such as love (1 John 4:17-18), endurance (James 1:4) and holiness (2 Cor. 7:1). Its progressive aspect is shown to us by these scriptures:

"... let us cleanse ourselves ... **perfecting holiness** in the fear of God." (2 Cor. 7:1)
"... are you now **being perfected** in the flesh?" (Gal. 3:3).
"... in understanding be perfect (1 Cor. 14:20).
"... and we all ... **are being changed** into His likeness from glory to glory (2 Cor. 3:18).

(iii) Ultimate perfection (future experience in the NEXT life)

This describes our condition when we have laid aside all earthly flesh and weights and have taken on the imperishable body we spoke about in Chapter One and enter fully into the Kingdom of God as subjects of an everlasting Kingdom, e.g.:

"Not as though I had already attained this (resurrection from the dead) or have already **been perfected** ... (Phil. 3:12).

You have come to Mount Zion ... to the spirits of just men **made perfect** ... (Heb. 12:22-23).

"... that they, without us, should not **be made perfect**." (Heb. 11:40).

The above three (3) meanings of perfection have been the normal interpretations of Christians in the past, and just about every verse speaking of mankind's perfection has been hammered into a shape that will make it fit under one of the three headings given. This often happens when man's reason cannot believe the plain Word of God (cf. Matt. 22:29).

There are a few verses that do NOT easily lend themselves to being so moulded and labelled but which require an interpretation somewhere between Relative (Progressive) perfection and Ultimate perfection. For example, what are we to do with our main text:

"Be perfect as your Heavenly Father is perfect." (Matt. 5:48).

Surely we cannot escape from this command to all mankind (the Jew first, and then the gentiles)? How are we to understand it? Firstly the Christian cannot discount the validity of this command to him or her simply because of their legal position in Christ; that would be to deny its plain meaning. Secondly, it cannot mean **relative perfection** because the measure required is the perfect perfection of the Father! Future? To apply this verse to only those who will share in the (first) resurrection of the just, still to come, seems quite indefensible. Surely it means to aim to be perfect NOW, not to simply aim to be perfect in the future. Reformation historian and theologian **Professor Francis Schaeffer** called this verse "an absolute," and he was right. We need a FOURTH LABEL which we shall call:–

(iv) EXPERIENTIAL PERFECTION (in THIS life-time)

Matt. 5:48 (above) is surely one of those verses which says what it means and means what it says, and no theological juggling or hammering can change that. Not only that, there are many other verses for which the plain meaning is clearly a command, exhortation or description for attaining EXPERIENTAL PERFECTION in THIS life-time. For example, when Paul talks about the Church being without spot or wrinkle or any such blemish (Eph. 5:27) many Bible students believe that the perfection of the Church so described is only due to its legal position of being justified by faith through the imputed righteousness of Christ. The reasoning goes something like this. "The Church cannot attain to be literally perfect without spot or wrinkle through its **own** sanctification program, so its perfection must be **Christ's** perfection legally imputed to it." It is a common error, of course, to choose what seems to be the best option doctrinally rather than the plain truth. Most of us do this when we operate with the mind of flesh rather than the mind of the Spirit (Rom 8:5-6). This doctrinal theory (above):

    (a)   imposes a doctrine upon the text;

(b) destroys the literal meaning and requirement of the text, and

(c) is not supported by the apostle Peter, who says exactly the same thing as Paul, but makes it plain that the perfection required by the Lord is not a positional or legal perfection but is to be EXPERIENCED by Christians (already positionally perfect) who are waiting for the NEW heavens and earth... (2 Peter 3:13-14).

The following scriptures need careful consideration:

1. EXPERIENTIAL PERFECTION? - THE IMMEDIATE AIM

* **Be perfect** as your Heavenly Father is (perfect) ... (Matt. 5:48).
* **... experience** what is ... perfect (Rom. 12:2).
* Yet among those who are perfect we speak wisdom (1 Cor. 2:6).
* ... in understanding be perfect (1 Cor. 14:20).
* **And His gifts were ... for the perfecting of the saints** (Eph. 4:12).
* Let us therefore, as many as be perfect ... (Phil. 3:15).
* ... that we may present every man perfect in Christ Jesus (Col. 1:28).
* ... that you may stand perfect and complete (Col. 4:12).
* ... in order that the man of God may be fitted ... (2 Tim. 3:17).
* But solid food is for the perfect ... (Heb. 5:14).
* ... **let us ... go on to perfection** (Heb. 6:1).
* ... that you may be perfect and entire, lacking in nothing (James 1:4).

156

(SINLESS PERFECTION?)

* All who remain in Jesus do not commit sin ... No one born of God commits sin ... he is not able to sin (1 John 3:6-9). *Comment: probably a reference to the New Man in Christ, in contrast with the Old Man, cause of all sins.*
* 1 Peter 2:21f. urges Christians to follow the example of Christ, who did no sin.
* ... whoever has suffered in the flesh (like Jesus) has ceased from sin (1 Peter 4:1). *Comment: probably a reference to the stigmata of Jesus (Gal. 6:17).*

2. YOUR RESTORATION PROGRAM COMMANDED BY THE WORD

* Be TRANSFORMED by the RESTORING of your mind so that you may EXPERIENCE what is ... perfect (Rom. 12:1-2).
* CLEANSE ourselves from ALL POLLUTION of flesh and spirit ... (2 Cor. 7:1).
* CLEANSE your hands, and PURIFY YOUR HEARTS (James 4:8).
* Purify yourself, as He is pure, if you want to see the Lord (1 John 3:2-3).
* Make straight the way of the Lord (Luke 3:4).
* CLEANSE YOURSELF and call on the Lord out of a PURE HEART (2 Tim. 2:21-22).
* Let us put away every obstacle and persistent, personal sin ... (Heb. 12:1).

3. THE MEASURE OF PERFECTION & RESTORATION—THE SON OF GOD—CHRIST JESUS.

* Because those whom He foreknew, He also PREDESTINED TO BE CONFORMED TO THE IMAGE

OF HIS SON, in order that He should be the proto-type among many brethren (Rom. 8:29).
* ... as we bore the image of the earthly man, we shall also bear the image of the heavenly man (1 Cor. 15:49).
* "We (Christians) ARE BEING CHANGED into His likeness (image) from glory into glory..." (2 Cor. 3:18).
* ... the Lord Jesus Christ, who will change the body of our humiliation to be conformed to His glorious body, according to the working of his power... (Philip. 3:21).
* ... we shall be like Him... (1 John 3:2).

4. THE GLORIOUS BRIDE HAS MADE HERSELF READY (Rev. 19:6-9, 21:2-4,9-11)—THE ULTIMATE GOAL

* The King's daughter is all glorious within (Ps. 45:13).
* You are altogether beautiful, my darling, and there is no blemish in you (Song of Songs 4:7).
* ... Let the Bridegroom come out of His chamber and the Bride out of her Bridal Chamber (Joel 2:16).
* ... that He might present to Himself the glorious church, not having spot or wrinkle or any such thing, that she might be holy and unblemished (Eph. 5:27).
* ... be diligent to be found by Him spotless and un-blemished (and) in peace (2 Peter 3:14).

THE CLIMAX   **1 Thess. 4:13-18**

So there we have it. The bottom, bottom line is to be per-fected like Jesus, the Son of God, so that when He comes for His Bride, THE BRIDE WILL BE LIKE HIM! (1 John 3:2) So this means we must be beautiful BEFORE He comes to collect us—**Now, in this life-time.** It means that End-time Deliverance is really God's RESTORA-TION PROGRAM for the whole human race. We were made in the image of God but when Adam and Eve fell from Grace the human race became polluted servants of satan, demonised by sin and death. However through the second Adam who is Jesus Christ (1 Cor. 15:45-50), and His victory over satan on the Cross, mankind has been given the opportunity for RESTORATION, **a FULL RESTORATION into the likeness of the perfect Son of God.**

It is mind-blowing, I know. The Apostle Paul expressed it so well when he quoted the prophet Isaiah (64:4).

> **"Eye has not seen, nor ear heard,**
> **nor the heart of man conceived, what**
> **God has prepared for those who love Him"**
> **(1 Cor. 2:9).**

The **offer**, through Christ Jesus, is to all mankind. The **application of the offer** is to those called to be in the Bride of Christ—those who have this hope and are purifying themselves (1 John 3:3).

OBJECTION

Some folk will say that **sinless perfection** is impossible. They will argue that *"if we say we have no* (disease of) *sin* (singular) *we deceive ourselves and the truth is not in us"* (1 John 1:8) but it is also true that Jesus came to take away (the disease of) the sin (singular) of the world (John 1:29). What the apostle John said about Christians who believe they have no (root disease of) sin was certainly right when he wrote it. It was also certainly right down through the centuries, but it may not be applicable for the prepared Bride, that is, the Rapture party who are caught up alive, without experiencing death. That is to say, although the Rapture party would have been born with the root of sin like everybody else, if they have purified themselves and made themselves ready then the Lord will have taken away their (roots of) sin BEFORE the trumpet sounds and we are caught up.

We know that *the wages of sin is death* (Rom. 6:23) and if the Rapture party is not going to taste death this infers **they will escape both the first (natural) and the second (spiritual) deaths,** because both the root of sin and the misdeeds of sins (plural) have been dealt with. In any event, if what John said worries you, then **do NOT say that you have no sin;** that is for the Lord alone to see and judge.

I personally would not dare say that sinless perfection was impossible in this End-Time (1 John 3:6-9, 1 Peter 4:1), because the Lord is just as likely to come back and say to me, *"With men it is impossible, but not with God; for all things are possible with God (Mark 10:27). You know neither the scriptures, nor the power of God!"* (Mark 12:24).

It is clear that we who wish to be at the Wedding Feast MUST be cleansed and purified INWARDLY, as the commands of the Word of God are issued to Blood-bought Christians. The goal—God's predestined will for us—is to be like Jesus (Rom. 8:29). Whether it is actually possible or not is not really the point. The point is that **we are to be as ready and as prepared as the Grace of God enables us to be,** without any reservation

160

whatsoever! What we have to keep in mind at all times is that we have a miracle-working God who delights to KEEP His Word to those who OBEY His Word.

We don't have to SAY anything about our condition but let us make sure our lamps are FULL OF OIL!

For further reading "A Plain Account of Christian Perfection" by John Wesley, as authorised by the Wesleyan Conference Office, London 1872 and reprinted by Beacon Hill Press of Kansas City. MO. U.S.A.

This book is produced by FULL SALVATION FEL-
LOWSHIP LTD., and designed to assist the people of
God in their preparation for the drama of the End Time,
which we believe has already begun on God's calendar.

The others published are:

"Guidance for Those Receiving Deliverance"
"The Re-incarnation Deception"
"Headcovering and Lady Pastor-Teachers"
"Christian Authority and Power"
Christian Deliverance:
    Book 1 **"Make Yourselves Ready"**
    Book 2 **"Engaging the Enemy"**
    Book 3 **"Walking in Victory"**
"Your Full Salvation"
"Surviving the Distress of Nations"

Others in the process of production and to be published
soon are:

"Toronto and the Truths You Haven't Heard Before!"
Christian Deliverance Book 4
"Discerning Human Nature"
"Sex, Demons and Morality"
"The Stigmata of Jesus"

Also "A Fresh Look" series on widely debated subjects,
such as:

"Baptism—Water and Spirit"
"Fullness and Tongues"

     *   *   *

162

TRADE ENQUIRIES

PUBLISHER—MALAYSIA

Bethlehem Publishers
Kuala Lumpur
Malaysia

UNITED KINGDOM
Sword Publications
P.O. Box 139
Aberdeen AB9 8LF
SCOTLAND

Tel: (1224) 480 294
Fax: (1224) 312 727

PHILIPPINES

The Good News of Jesus Christ Fellowship Inc.
P.O Box 6
CAGAYAN DE ORO CITY
9000 PHILIPPINES

U. S. A.

Impact Christian Books, Inc.
332 Leffingwell Ave, Suite 101
Kirkwood
Mo 63122
U. S. A.

Tel: (314) 822 3309
Fax: (314) 822 3325

AFRICA

SJBS Outreach Inc.
P.O. Box 4953 Oshodi
Lagos, NIGERIA
WEST AFRICA

Full Salvation Ministry
P.O. Box 3438 KISII
KENYA, E.AFRICA

Tel: 381 31319

AUSTRALIA. TRADE AND MINISTRY ENQUIRES TO:
Full Salvation Fellowship Ltd.
P. O. Box 1020
Crows Nest, 2065
AUSTRALIA
Tel: (02) 9436 3657   Fax: (02) 9437 6700

MORE COMMENTS

I have been greatly encouraged by certain sharings in your book "End-Time Deliverance"...

(Miss) Ida Kueh
East Malaysia.

I find "End-Time Deliverance" very good teaching.

Pastor Jean-Claude Soupin
Quatre-Bornes, **Mauritius.**

Praise God for the wonderful revelations based on the Word of God for these last days.

Dr Rajan J. Nathaniel
Sri Lanka.

Just finished reading "End-Time Deliverance" and was led to several revelations from the Holy Spirit—confirming your words. I stand amazed and wonderful enlightenment floods me...

Art Abrom
New Jersey, **U.S.A.**

When I read "End-Time deliverance" I was blessed by your message and led to impart the truth to my Church.

Pastor Rene T. Salazar
Iligan City, **PHILIPPINES.**

"We are enjoying your books which give such a practical approach to this ministry... We would welcome some affiliation with you... as there is no (other) Fellowship in Israel engaged in Deliverance."

Alan & Helena Friedman, **Jerusalem.**